LIFE LESSONS FROM DAVID

Study by Robert G. Baker
Commentary by Hardy Clemons

Free downloadable Teaching Guide for this study available at
NextSunday.com/teachingguides

NextSunday Resources
6316 Peake Road
Macon, Georgia 31210-3960
1-800-747-3016
©2012 by NextSunday Resources

The paper used in this publication meets the minimum requirements of
American National Standard for Information Sciences—
Permanence of Paper for Printed Library Materials.
ANSI Z39.48–1984. (alk. paper)

All Scripture quotations are from the New Revised Standard Version of the
Bible copyright © 1989 by the Division of Christian Education of the National Council of
Churches of Christ in the USA.

Library of Congress Cataloging-in-Publication Data

CIP Information on file.

TABLE OF CONTENTS

Life Lessons from David

Study Introduction 1

Lesson 1 The Adolescent David: Waging the Battles of Giant Proportions
         1 Samuel 17:1-51
         Study 3
         Commentary 13

Lesson 2 The Adult David: Dancing Before the Lord
         2 Samuel 6:1-15
         Study 21
         Commentary 31

Lesson 3 The Midlife David: Frustrated and Foolish
         2 Samuel 11
         Study 39
         Commentary 49

Lesson 4 The Senior Adult David: Passing on a Legacy
         1 Kings 1:1–2:12
         Study 57
         Commentary 67

HOW TO USE THIS STUDY

NextSunday Resources Adult Bible Studies are designed to help adults study Scripture seriously within the context of the larger Christian tradition and, through that process, find their faith renewed, challenged, and strengthened. We study the Scriptures because we believe they affect our current lives in important ways. Each study contains the following three components:

Study Guide

Each study guide lesson is arranged in five movements:

Reflecting recalls a contemporary story, anecdote, example, or illustration to help us anticipate the session's relevance in our lives.

Remembering provides a frame of reference for the Scriptures.

Studying is centered on giving the biblical material in-depth attention while often surrounding it with helpful insights from theology, ethics, church history, and other areas.

Understanding helps us find relevant connections between our lives and the biblical message.

What About Me? provides brief statements that help unite life issues with the meaning of the biblical text.

Commentary

Each study guide lesson is accompanied by an additional, in-depth commentary on the biblical material. Written by a different author than the study guide, each commentary gives the opportunity for learners to approach the Scripture text from a separate but complementary viewpointt.

Teaching Guide

In addition to the provided study guide and commentary, *NextSunday Resources* also provides a *free* downloadable teaching guide, available at NextSunday.com. Each teaching guide gives the teacher tools for focusing on the content of each study guide lesson through additional commentary and Bible background information. Through teacher helps and teaching options, each teaching guide also provides substance for variety and choice in the preparation of each lesson.

NextSunday
Resources

STUDY INTRODUCTION

From the time I first heard of David and Goliath, I've been "hooked" on David. Several elements of his story have caught my attention.

First is the huge amount of biblical material devoted to David: the stories about the "human" David (1 and 2 Samuel); the more "idealized" interpretation of David's reign in 1 Chronicles; and the post-Davidic references to David in the books of 1 and 2 Kings. Combine these David stories and references with the numerous psalms attributed to David, as well as the New Testament passages where Jesus is referred to as the "Son of David," and you will see the massive amount of Scripture that is devoted to Israel's second and greatest king.

A second element is the high regard biblical writers placed on David and his rule. The overall biblical evaluation of David is "ideal" king (1 Sam 13:14). David's reign was regarded as the "Golden Age"—so golden that the Israelites viewed the coming messiah as one who would be a "son of David" and establish a new Davidic-like kingdom on earth.

A third element that lures me to David is that despite the mostly "ideal" treatment David receives, many Scriptures (2 Sam 9–20) offer a candid and human portrayal of him. Adultery, attempted cover-ups, murder, and conflict with his adult children are a few of David's "sins."

This "human" description of David relates to a fourth surprising "catch"—namely, God loved and used David in spite of his sins. If forgiveness and hope were available to David, they surely exist for us.

John Claypool has helped me notice another aspect of David's story. In the Bible, we catch David in the various stages of the human journey: childhood, adolescence, adulthood, and senior adulthood. From the biblical treatment of the stages of David's life, we can land some insights to assist us in better understanding the human journey.

So I invite you to join me as we cast a few "lines and lures" into the sea of biblical material about David. Specifically, we'll "fish" a bit in the waters of David's adolescence, adulthood, midlife, and senior adult years. With a little "luck," perhaps we will "catch" enough from David's story to make our own human journeys more successful and fulfilling. May God be with us as the "Lord was with David" (1 Sam 16:18)!

THE ADOLESCENT DAVID: WAGING BATTLES OF GIANT PROPORTIONS

1 Samuel 17:1-51

Central Question

What are some of the "giants" you are battling?

Scripture

1 Samuel 17:42-49 When the Philistine looked and saw David, he disdained him, for he was only a youth, ruddy and handsome in appearance. 43 The Philistine said to David, "Am I a dog, that you come to me with sticks?" And the Philistine cursed David by his gods. 44 The Philistine said to David, "Come to me, and I will give your flesh to the birds of the air and to the wild animals of the field." 45 But David said to the Philistine, "You come to me with sword and spear and javelin; but I come to you in the name of the LORD of hosts, the God of the armies of Israel, whom you have defied. 46 This very day the LORD will deliver you into my hand, and I will strike you down and cut off your head; and I will give the dead bodies of the Philistine army this very day to the birds of the air and to the wild animals of the earth, so that all the earth may know that there is a God in Israel, 47 and that all this assembly may know that the LORD does not save by sword and spear; for the battle is the LORD's and he will give you into our hand." 48 When the Philistine drew nearer to meet David, David ran quickly toward the battle line to meet the Philistine. 49 David put his hand in his bag, took out a stone, slung it, and struck the Philistine on his forehead; the stone sank into his forehead, and he fell face down on the ground.

Reflecting

I had not met him in person, yet our phone conversations and his résumé caused me to look forward to his interview. After all, I was an avid sports fan, and David had been a recent letterman on the University of Kentucky football team. In my mind, I had already pictured what this "David" would look like and imagined what type of youth minister he would be.

Imagine my surprise when he arrived for the interview. In walked a 5'6", no-more-than-160-pound guy with thinning hair. "Hi, I'm Dave!" he said. "Oh," I thought, trying to hide my disappointment.

"Hi," I quickly attempted to recover. "I'm Bob, the pastor here. So you played football for the Kentucky Wildcats?"

"Sure did," Dave answered. "I was a walk-on wide receiver. I played on the scout team and finally earned a scholarship. I even got in on a few plays in a real game my senior year."

"How did this guy survive four years of college football?" I wondered. But before the interview was over, I knew the answer. Dave's motto was, "Be the best!" With God's help, coupled with an uncanny work ethic and healthy self-esteem, Dave constantly sought to be the best football player/youth minister/staff member/disciple of Jesus Christ that he could be!

Dave "wowed" us in that interview. He had an incredible knowledge of youth ministry. He was humble, yet confident. His enthusiasm for life was contagious. He won the hearts of the search committee, was offered the job, and soon won the hearts of not only our young people, but our entire church.

Over the years, Dave daily sought to "be the best" he could be. He encountered battles with several giants, including the death of his mother. Even when "wounded," he never gave up. With God's help, this "David" slew many giants, won many battles, and inspired church members to "keep on keeping on" and to "be the best" that we could be with the Lord's help. This David, the once adolescent, is now very much an adult follower of Jesus Christ, a "man after God's own heart."

Remembering

Our text is part of a larger block of Scripture from 1 Samuel 16–2 Samuel 5 that scholars regard as "The History of David's Rise," which traces David from a shepherd boy to his establishment as the king of Israel.

David's victory over Goliath played an instrumental role in David's rise to kingship. More specifically, the David versus Goliath story is a pivotal episode in the ancient rivalry between the Philistines and the Israelites. By the time of today's text, Philistine soldiers were deep in Israelite territory (1 Sam 4–6). Indeed, fear of the Philistines had been a primary motivating factor in the Israelites' demand to have a king (1 Sam 8). As Israel's first king, regardless of how well he led Israel against other foes, Saul lived with the daily pressure that the Israelites expected him to defeat the Philistines.

The tension between these rival peoples dates back at least as far as 1150 BC when judges such as Samson led the Israelites against the Philistines (Judg 13–16; Katzenstein, 328).

According to John Claypool, adolescence is "the transitional period between the dependency of childhood and the independency of adulthood" (40). In 1 Samuel 17, David is in the "in-between" stage of childhood and adulthood. Although the youngest of eight sons, Jesse trusted David to care for the sheep. However, at the beginning of 1 Samuel 17, David is relegated to the role of "messenger boy," whose task is to visit three of his older soldier brothers who are on the battlefield and to report back to his father.

David's journey to the battlefield resulted in much more than a "here's-a-care-package-from-home-and-how-are-you-doing?" visit with his brothers. David engaged in a battle in which he not only faced the giant Philistine warrior Goliath, but his own "stage of life" battle of leaving adolescence and entering adulthood. By the end of chapter 17, the adolescent David has made significant strides in becoming an adult. Moreover, the God who helped him in the battle with the giant Goliath also helped him in his struggles with the giant challenges of growing up—

challenges that seem especially difficult during the "in-between" stage of life known as adolescence.

Studying

The setting for today's text is the Valley of Elah, fifteen miles southwest of Bethlehem. The Philistine army has gathered on a mountain on one side of the valley while the Israelite troops, under King Saul, have encamped on the opposite mountainside (1 Sam 17:1-3).

• *Goliath's challenge (vv. 4-11)*. Goliath, the gigantic champion of the Philistine army, appealed to an ancient tradition known as representative combat. Goliath would fight "one-on-one" against anyone chosen by King Saul to represent Israel. If the Israelite representative defeated Goliath, then the Philistine army would become the servants of Israel. However, if the heavily favored Goliath emerged as the victor, then the Israelites must agree to become servants of the Philistines.

Goliath has been touted as having been 6'9" (Brueggemann, *First and Second Samuel*, 127). Others who use the "cubit" system have speculated that Goliath's height could have been as much as 9'6" (Philbeck, 53). Whatever his actual height, Goliath's towering appearance successfully intimi-

A cubit was regarded as the distance from the elbow to the top of the middle finger—usually about seventeen to eighteen inches—while a span was the distance between the little finger and one's fully extended thumb—around eight inches.

dated Saul and his troops. In addition, Goliath's daily verbal challenges and insults further "psyched out" the fear-paralyzed Israelite army (vv. 11, 23-24). The Philistine champion essentially immobilized the Israelites with his intimidation tactics before the battle ever began!

• *David's response (vv. 12-30)*. While visiting with his older brothers, David heard one of Goliath's challenges. The shepherd was shocked that no one would respond to the challenge. The Israelites (including David's brothers) fled in fear whenever Goliath approached (vv. 23-24).

"What's wrong with you?" David purportedly asked the Israelite soldiers (v. 26). David—in what can be regarded as a classic expression of adolescent idealism—indicated his willingness to fight the giant. This "adolescent" David not only dared to face Goliath, but he was also brash enough to reprimand his brothers, the other soldiers, and ultimately King Saul. "Do you believe in a living God or not?" David chided his fellow Israelites. "If you do, then act like it!" (vv. 26-30).

• *Saul's decision (vv. 31-37).* News of David's willingness to face Goliath spread rapidly throughout the Israelite camp and soon reached King Saul, who summoned David. In a somewhat more official manner, David offered his service: "Oh King, let no one's heart fail because of Goliath and his challenge; I will go and fight against him" (v. 32).

It is significant that both speeches attributed to David in 1 Samuel 17 point beyond David and his own abilities to God (Brueggemann, *David's Truth*, 35). While speaking to Saul, David declared, "The LORD...will save me from the hand of the Philistine" (v. 37). And when confronting Goliath, David exclaimed, "You come to me with sword and spear and javelin; but I come to you in the name of the LORD of hosts...whom you have defied. This very day, the LORD will deliver you into my hand" (vv. 45-46).

Initially, Saul rejected David's offer (v. 33). David, however, responded to Saul by sharing several items from the "previous experience" section of his "résumé," declaring how as a shepherd he had killed lions and bears (vv. 34-36). David's "résumé" impressed Saul. Time was running out for the Israelite army. This young David was better prepared for battle than Saul had originally thought!

Perhaps what ultimately motivated Saul to send David into battle, however, was the personal testimony that he so confidently shared with the king: "The LORD, who saved me from the paw of the lion and from the paw of the bear, will save me from the hand of this Philistine" (v. 37). Saul was convinced. David would be the Israelite representative against the Philistine champion. Having been reminded not to leave the Lord out of life's crucial decisions, Saul told David, "Go, and may the LORD be with you!" (v. 37).

• *Preparing for battle (vv. 38-40).* Saul attempted to prepare his young protégé for battle by clothing him in his own armor. David found that what worked for Saul was not a good fit for him (v. 39). Removing Saul's armor, David chose to battle Goliath with his own equipment—his staff, five smooth stones, and his sling.

• *David versus Goliath (vv. 41-51b).* As Goliath approached, he tauntingly remarked about David's youth and lack of appropriate battle equipment. Goliath arrogantly vowed to decimate the young shepherd and to feed David's remains "to the birds of the air and to the wild animals of the field" (v. 44).

David remained undaunted. Continuing, he confidently answered Goliath: "This very day the LORD will deliver you into my hand...so that all the earth may know that there is a God in Israel" (vv. 45-47).

Swiftly transforming his words into action, David put one of the smooth stones into his sling and let it fly. His shot struck Goliath, sinking into his forehead. The Philistine champion fell to the ground, overcome and killed by the adolescent David.

Realizing that their champion had fallen, the Philistine army fled from the scene. The Israelite troops, obviously emboldened by David's stunning upset win, pursued the Philistines and drove them outside of Israelite territory. Thanks largely to the faith and courage of David, the Israelites won a momentous victory over their Philistine rivals—a victory that launched the previously unknown David into the limelight of Israelite history (1 Sam 18:6-8).

The encounter between David and Goliath is regarded as one of the greatest battles of all time. This well-known story has been analyzed repeatedly. Several insights enhance our understanding: (1) In the initial conversation between David and Saul (vv. 31-40), David spoke first. Custom dictated that the king should have been the first to speak. Unbeknownst to Saul, however, the Lord had already chosen David as Israel's new king (1 Sam 16:12-13). Having David speak first further demonstrated David's rise to kingship (Brueggemann, *First and Second Samuel*, 129). Having

David speak first may also underscore the emergence of David from adolescence to adulthood.

(2) David called on the name of the Lord (v. 37). Only after David referred to God's personal name (Yahweh) did Saul have the courage to speak the Lord's name. David alone recognized that God was the real source of the Israelites' courage. Saul and his troops felt that they needed to face Goliath on Goliath's terms—sword, spear, and armor. The "adolescent" David reminded Saul, Israel, and us that the ultimate resource for confronting life's giants is the Lord (Brueggemann, *First and Second Samuel*, 130-31). In the area of faith development, the "adolescent" David of 1 Samuel 17 was more adult-like than the cowering Israelite soldiers and the indecisive, ineffective King Saul!

Understanding

The conversation between David and Saul (vv. 31-40) has been described as "a classic interaction between an emerging adolescent and the older generation" (Claypool, 45). This interaction is characterized initially by the tension expected between an eager adolescent (David) and a hesitant, if not reluctant, adult guardian (Saul). David expressed certainty in his ability to assume responsibility for his own actions. While not disowning the adult figures in his life (Jesse and Saul), David was convinced that he was mature enough to assume the adult-sized task of confronting the giant. Saul, on the other hand, initially questioned David's readiness to face the "giants" of adulthood by battling the Philistine champion (v. 33).

Finally, Saul gave David permission to take on adulthood. Still, Saul found that "letting David go" was difficult, so he attempted to do what many parent figures attempt to do when "sending" their children into the fray of battling adulthood giants—to "load David down with his own armor" (v. 38; Claypool, 46). David wisely realized that he could not successfully enter adulthood with someone else's armor. David needed his own armor—his own faith, convictions, and beliefs. He could and did learn much from Saul and Jesse, but he could not be Saul or

Jesse. David could only emerge into adulthood and effectively battle the giants of life by being David.

First Samuel 17 offers guidance for both adolescents and caring adults, yet this text is about far more than "coming of age." This story provides insights for all of God's followers who at various stages in our life journeys find some situational giant standing directly in our path!

Throughout our lives, we engage in battles with disease, death, and grief. We wrestle with doubt, temptation, peer pressure. Some of us have bouts with family troubles, vocational problems, and financial concerns. There are many "giants" in our lives with which we do battle. Like David, we are often the underdogs in such confrontations.

Do we dare trust in God to help us use our talents when we face the Goliaths of life? Do we allow the giants we face to paralyze us with fear? Do our lives point beyond ourselves and our own abilities to our trust in the living God?

What is the "game plan" for facing such giants? David's answer: "Trust in God!" (v. 26). How ironic that we who profess to follow God often neglect to trust God! We tend, like Goliath, to trust too much in ourselves and our own resources. We try, like Saul with his preoccupation on the "world's armor," to outdo Goliath on Goliath's terms. This is certainly not to de-emphasize helping ourselves by developing and using our own gifts and talents. David was by no means shy about putting his abilities into practice. However, what empowered David to help himself was his trust in the living God.

We don't win every fight with giants, and neither did David. But even through lost battles, God provides us with strength and guidance. Most importantly, even through battles we lose, we who trust in God know that the ultimate victory belongs to the Lord: "For I am convinced that nothing—neither death, nor life, nor angels, nor rulers, nor powers, [nor any 'giant' that I face whatsoever]—will be able to separate us from the love of the living God" (Rom 8:38-39).

What About Me?

- *God is drawn to the underdog.* Just because you are not favored by the majority does not mean that you will not be favored by God. In 1 Samuel 17, God assists the young David. In other passages, it is the poor, the prisoner, the blind, the lame, the leper, the widow, and the tax collector whom God helps. Surely those of us who follow God should be involved along with God in giving a chance to underdogs!

- *Dare to be yourself.* When Saul attempted to send David into battle with his armor, David opted for a radical alternative—he dared to be himself. There always are those who will attempt to force conformity, to persuade you to act and believe just like everyone else. Yet have you ever found yourself succumbing to peer pressure and group conform-ity because you wanted to be accepted? Pretending to be something that you are not may temporarily enhance the impression that you make on others, but in the heat of a battle with giants, pretense and appearances are not very helpful.

- *Battling giants is not devoid of wounds, setbacks, and even defeats.* David's willingness to fight against the giant was not without obstacles (vv. 28-30, 33, 41-44). Just because God is with us when we battle giants does not mean that such battles will be without struggle.

- *Trust in God as your ultimate resource.* Despite his extraordinary natural abilities, David knew the folly of attempting to face Goliath on his own. Indeed, David's trust in God empowered the young shepherd to use his own resources. Do we have that kind of trust in the Lord, who enables us to face our fears and to minister in spite of obstacles? What are we attempting to do in our lives and in our churches that will not be accomplished unless we trust in God as our ultimate resource? Are we trying to "outdo Goliath on Goliath's terms"? Do we really trust in a living God?

• *The passage from adolescence to adulthood is part of God's plan.* The adolescent stage of the human journey is not without struggles for both the developing adolescent and the parent/parent figure. In fact, someone has remarked that adolescence offers "something painful for everybody." However, in spite of the seemingly all-but-impossible challenges, this adolescent segment of the human saga is normal. Furthermore, and most importantly, the God whose plan for human beings includes adolescence does not abandon us during this stage of the human journey. The Lord who was constantly "with David" is always with us even when we are going through the adolescent phase of life.

Resources

Walter Brueggemann, *David's Truth in Israel's Imagination & Memory* (Philadelphia: Fortress Press, 1985).

———, *First and Second Samuel,* Interpretation: A Bible Commentary for Teaching and Preaching (Louisville: John Knox Press, 1990).

John Claypool, *Stages: The Art of Living the Expected* (Waco: Word Books, 1980).

H. J. Katzenstein, "Philistines," *The Anchor Bible Dictionary*, vol. 5 (New York: Doubleday, 1992).

Ben Philbeck Jr., "1–2 Samuel," *The Broadman Bible Commentary*, vol. 3 (Nashville: Broadman Press, 1970).

THE ADOLESCENT DAVID: WAGING BATTLES OF GIANT PROPORTIONS

1 Samuel 17:1-51

Introduction

It's not just adolescents who wage battles of giant proportions. We all do. Yet, how easy it is for adults to discount the gravity of adolescent battles—as was done repeatedly with David? Moreover, we tend to understate both the power and competence youth bring to battles.

We can learn a lot from David in his walk with God—if we are willing to read, listen, discuss with each other, ponder, and pay attention to the wisdom the Scripture offers us.

First, we will consider David as a teen—moving from childhood into adulthood. Next week, we see him as an adult, facing the challenges and joys of being his own person. Third, we see him struggling with the frustrations, temptations, grief, and guilt of midlife. Finally, we see him facing the challenges of aging.

John Claypool's *The Saga of Life: Living Gracefully through the Stages* uses David as a paradigm for exploring the stages of human life because "more material is contained in Holy Scripture about the different phases of his life than of any other individual" ([New Orleans: Insight Press, 2003] 20).

I. David's Prelude to Battle, 1 Sam 15–16.

To understand David, we must review his being chosen *by God* through *Samuel*. Samuel grieved over Saul's spiritual disintegration (1 Sam 15:34). Saul's disintegration kept him fixed more on what he and Israel had lost than on God's vision for the future. God had exciting plans for Israel with David as king. First

Samuel 15–17 provides a wider context of David's preparation to fight Goliath.

God addressed Samuel, saying, "How long will you continue to grieve over Saul?" (16:1). God is not saying that grief is bad or unnecessary, but a time comes in our grief when it is mandatory to make the painful choice to leave the past and its hurts behind so we can move into the present and future that God has planned.

A prelude to Goliath's story is that of Samuel coming to Jesse's house to qualify his sons. God had said, "I have provided for myself a king among his sons" (16:1), but as Samuel looked at the sons present, God repeatedly said, "This is not the one. Humans look on the outward appearance, but God looks on the heart" (16:7).

Seven sons stood before Samuel, and still no king was evident. What a key insight to spiritual power this is! Strength is more spiritual than physical! Humans get fixated on externals. We tend to think that everything is better if it is bigger. We assume that if we have the biggest size and best high-tech equipment, we are assured of victory in any venue. God, on the other hand, leads us to engage the internal spiritual power of life through a healthy relationship with God, our neighbors, and ourselves. In other words, being spiritual involves knowing who God really is as well as who we really are.

Samuel asked in mystery, "Are there yet no sons?" Jesse replied reluctantly, "Well, uh, yes, but, uh, he's just a kid. He's out keeping the sheep" (my translation). In other words, he didn't see any reason why the young kid should have come in (16:11).

However, Samuel declared, "We won't proceed until he's here. Go get him!" When David entered, God said, "David is the one." Samuel discovered God's new king through the spiritual process of worship, not the political process of power brokering.

II. Discounts to Self We Face

We are all vulnerable to being "disdained" (17:42) by external and internal forces. Consider some forces that devalued David:

• His father, in not thinking he was important enough for the gathering for worship with all the brothers (16:3)

- His brothers and their comrades (17:28-30)
- Saul ("You are not able...for you are but a youth!" 17:33)
- Goliath disdained this young "whipper-snapper" (17:42)

Yet David, in his relationship with God, which was nurtured on those lonely sojourns in the field, had developed a strong and valid ego rooted in God! Plus, he had developed his own skills for battle. A sturdy ego plus well-developed skills equals a mighty spiritual arsenal.

We must use the word "ego" carefully. Hans Selye said there is a difference between being "ego-istic" and "ego-tistic" (Pastoral Conference on Stress, The Galt House, Louisville, KY, 1980). To be ego*tistic* is to be self-centered, self-absorbed, self-seeking. To be ego*istic* is to have a valid assessment of self, a firm ego, neither too high nor too low an opinion. Paul speaks of this blend of ego strength when he calls for "a sober judgment of self according to the measure of faith which God has assigned" (Rom 12:3).

When Paul urged believers to know and use their God-given gifts, I think of young David. His view of himself proved accurate—neither too high nor too low a self-image. David's self was centered in relationship with God; he was in tune with the gifted person God had created him to be. Others disdained him, and doubtless, he struggled some with issues of self-confidence. However, when he faced this gigantic battle with Goliath, he was confident "according to the measure of faith God had given." He was a true individual and a true follower of God. He knew what Zechariah would articulate years later—that it is "not by might nor by power, but by my Spirit says the God of hosts"—that we wage such battles (Zech 4:6).

III. Giants We Face

Some might say that we just don't understand the size of the particular battle *they* face. Or they may be focused on the battle rather than the strength God can give to wage such warfare. Consider the personal size and equipment that Goliath brought to the fight!

The Philistines had a hero named Goliath...who was over nine feet tall. He wore a bronze helmet and had bronze armor to protect his chest and legs. The chest armor alone weighed 125 pounds...and his spear was so big that the iron spearhead alone weighed more than 15 pounds. (17:4-7, Contemporary English Version).

The point here is that Goliath was not only massive, but that he also had the best technology of war that could possibly be assembled—both offensively and defensively. Furthermore, it is important to remember that when we are engaged in battle of any kind, the foe *always* seems massive and daunting. Plus, it is easy to underestimate one's own power and resourcefulness in facing such a fearsome enemy. Overestimating the enemy plus underestimating what we can do with God's strength and our own giftedness equals a battle that seems more daunting than it may actually be!

We all have major battles to fight. Teens struggle with a way to seem older and cooler, to be given responsibility and freedom. Young adults agonize with the need to achieve and excel to feed their ego, to catch up and keep up. Mid-adults face the squeezes of the "sandwich generation" when they are caught between the needs and demands of their children and their aging parents. Older adults vie with feelings that we don't matter anymore, that we aren't contributing, or with fears of being a burden to our children, or not having enough at the end.

It is easy to "throw in the towel" when we get fixated on the power of the enemy. That is exactly where Saul, David's brothers, and the Israelite army focused: *"THIS battle is too much for us!"* Your list may seem the same way: *I don't have the strength!*

Not having the strength is precisely the point. We human beings don't have this kind of strength—except for the power of God. We must always remember that power from God *is* available.

IV. Resources for Waging the Battle

Once David had enumerated his resources for the battle and why he thought he could defeat Goliath, Saul gave him his own armor. David could hardly move and he surely could not fight. Nor can we fight our own battle in someone else's armor. David had resources Saul didn't consider. We may have resources we aren't considering.

Setting aside fears, David called upon his own resources, which had more to do with spiritual trust than with confidence in superior weapons or abundant strength. Please note three things:

(1) David claimed the name of Yahweh—God's personal name: "You come to me with a sword, spear and javelin; but I come to you in the name of the LORD of Hosts whom you have defied" (17:45).

Biblical believers did not agree with the Shakespearean assessment that "a rose by any other name would smell as sweet." They attached the name of a person to the *being* of a person—including God. When God said to Moses, "My name is I Am," he was indicating that God is who God is and we are who we are as creations of God. To come in the name of God, as Moses did to Pharaoh or as David did to Goliath, is to come in the *authority* of God and with the *strength* of God (see W. Lee Humphreys' article on "Names," in *The Mercer Dictionary of the Bible*, ed. Watson E. Mills et al. [Macon GA: Mercer University Press, 1990] 602-603).

We do not fight our battles alone. As Martin Luther wrote in his great hymn "A Mighty Fortress Is Our God,"

> Did we in our own strength confide,
> Our striving would be losing;
> Were not the right Man on our side,
> The Man of God's own choosing.
> Dost ask who that may be?
> Christ Jesus, it is he;
> Lord Sabaoth his name,
> From age to age the same,
> And he must win the battle.

(2) David remembered times in even his own brief past when he had faced giant battles successfully in the strength of God.

Note that Goliath was fighting in his own strength, with great confidence in the invulnerable technology of his weapons. David was fighting for God's cause more than his own or Israel's. Moreover, he was armed with the power of the name of God. And he had weapons and skills he had learned as a shepherd boy. (3) David used tools that fit him. He also used strengths and skills he had developed as he grew to this stage. He went to fight the giant from his own center of confidence and faith, with his own implements, which weren't exactly high-tech. David used the simple tools of battle that he had honed against lions and bears— predators on his father's sheep. He waged his battle in the name of Yahweh!

In summary, we face giant battles much as David did. We have the same God to strengthen us. We have the same memory of times we were frightened out of our minds in the face of some huge foe. We have tools at our disposal we can call on from the armory of our personal and spiritual development. In the name and power of God, we can address even massive foes and prevail.

The "bottom line" is more than a number here. The battle is not about size or superior tools of war. It is not about getting what we want for our selfishness. It is not about being "number 1."

The bottom line is that we can draw on the strength of God and the skills God has helped us develop—no matter our age. God is the one who saves.

Notes

Notes

2

THE ADULT DAVID:
DANCING BEFORE THE LORD

2 Samuel 6:1-15

Central Question

Is God at the center of your worship?

Scripture

2 Samuel 6:1-15 David again gathered all the chosen men of Israel, thirty thousand. 2 David and all the people with him set out and went from Baale-judah, to bring up from there the ark of God, which is called by the name of the LORD of hosts who is enthroned on the cherubim. 3 They carried the ark of God on a new cart, and brought it out of the house of Abinadab, which was on the hill. Uzzah and Ahio, the sons of Abinadab, were driving the new cart 4 with the ark of God; and Ahio went in front of the ark. 5 David and all the house of Israel were dancing before the LORD with all their might, with songs and lyres and harps and tambourines and castanets and cymbals. 6 When they came to the threshing floor of Nacon, Uzzah reached out his hand to the ark of God and took hold of it, for the oxen shook it. 7 The anger of the LORD was kindled against Uzzah; and God struck him there because he reached out his hand to the ark; and he died there beside the ark of God. 8 David was angry because the LORD had burst forth with an outburst upon Uzzah; so that place is called Perez-uzzah, to this day. 9 David was afraid of the LORD that day; he said, "How can the ark of the LORD come into my care?" 10 So David was unwilling to take the ark of the LORD into his care in the city of David; instead David took it to the house of Obed-edom the Gittite. 11 The ark of the LORD remained in the house of Obed-edom the Gittite three months; and the LORD blessed Obed-edom and all his household. 12 It was told King David, "The LORD has blessed the household of Obed-edom and all that belongs to him, because of the ark of God." So David went and brought up the ark of God from the house of Obed-edom to the city of David with rejoicing; 13 and when those who bore the ark of the LORD had gone six paces, he sacrificed an ox and a fatling. 14 David danced before the LORD with all his might; David was girded with a linen ephod. 15 So David and all the house of Israel brought up the ark of the LORD with shouting, and with the sound of the trumpet.

Reflecting

In his book *Leadership That Works*, Leith Anderson defines leadership as "figuring out what needs to be done and then doing it!" (51). However, such leadership requires wisdom and maturity, because great leaders do what's best for the group they lead.

David is regarded as one of the greatest leaders in Israelite history. Aside from his relationship with God, one of his primary leadership gifts was being mature enough to determine what needed to happen and then taking the necessary actions to make it happen.

At the beginning of David's reign, a nation divided politically, geographically, and religiously needed unification. In selecting Jerusalem as the new capital city and transferring the ancient ark of the covenant to Jerusalem, David provided the foundation for both the political and religious unity that Israel so desperately needed. David, after "figuring out what needed to be done," set about to do it!

Remembering

Second Samuel 6 is actually the concluding segment of what scholars call the Ark Narrative (1 Sam 4:1–7:2; 2 Sam 6). The earlier portions of this story relate how the Philistines captured the ark after defeating the Israelites in battle. However, when these Philistine cities were struck with a deadly plague, the

Philistines attributed their misfortune to the presence of the ark and returned it to Israelite territory (1 Sam 6:13). Throughout the reign of King Saul, the ark remained in the care of the household of Abinadab, far removed from the center of Israelite life.

Keep in mind that David was a "southern boy" who was born and raised in the southern village of Bethlehem.

In today's text, David is the king of Israel. Israel was then composed of two distinct factions: Judah in the south and Israel in the north. At first, David was only the king at Hebron in the south (2 Sam 2:4). It was not until seven years later that the northern tribes of Israel also anointed David as their king (2 Sam 5:3).

Upon becoming king of both Judah and Israel, David and his troops marched to Jerusalem—a neutral territory that was the last remaining town

Second Samuel 5:4-5 summarizes the "split" nation over which David reigned: "David was thirty years old when he began to reign, and he reigned forty years. At Hebron, he reigned over Judah seven years and six months; and at Jerusalem he reigned over all Israel and Judah thirty-three years."

still occupied by the Canaanites, known as Jebusites. David's army defeated the Jebusites, and Jerusalem literally became "the city of David" (2 Sam 5:6-10). David wisely made the neutral Jerusalem, also geographically located between Israel and Judah, his headquarters and the political capital of the new "united" nation of Israel.

David realized, however, that political unification alone would not be sufficient. The people of Israel needed to be united religiously as well. Consequently, David sought to promote Jerusalem as the religious center by moving the ancient ark of the covenant there. Our text for today is the story of the ark's transfer to Jerusalem, which was a time for celebration and worship.

By this time, David is an adult. Not only is he older chronologically, but he has also made an important "developmental move" often associated with adulthood—namely, the move "from the infantile need to have everything serve him to the maturity of genuinely wanting to serve others" (Claypool, 64).

David could have made his own headquarters in the southern city of Hebron. However, in an effort to unify the nation, David demonstrated the maturity of an adult by working to "become part of the answer instead of part of the problem and contribute something positive to the stream of history" (Ibid., 65).

David's decision to transfer the ark to the new capital of Jerusalem also proved a mature one. Under King Saul, the ark (and possibly God) was relegated to the back burner of Israelite life. By moving the ark to the new capital, David was making a strategically important statement—namely, that his administration would strive to keep the Lord at the center of Israelite life. David opted to view kingship as an opportunity for him (and his fellow Israelites) to serve God.

Studying

• *The "return" of the ark: the procession begins (2 Sam 6:1-5).* David and his entourage journeyed to the house of Abinadab in Kiriath-jearim where the ark had been kept. The "cherubim" (v. 2) refer to the winged, angel-like creatures that adorned the cover of the ark (Ex 25:17-22). It was believed that the outstretched wings of these cherubim provided the "throne" upon which the invisible God was symbolically seated (Anderson, *2 Samuel*, 102). In this sense, the ark was perceived to be the portable throne for God and signified the Lord's presence wherever it was transported. Now the ark was being transported to Jerusalem where God would rightfully be recognized as the center of Israelite life! This was a joyful, momentous occasion. No wonder David and all the Israelites "were making merry

"Baalejudah" (v. 2) was possibly another name for the town of Kiriath-jearim or perhaps not a place name at all but an expression meaning "rulers of Judah" (Philbeck, 101).

with all their might" (v. 5) as they participated in this seven-mile religious parade.

Uzzah and Ahio, the sons or possibly even the grandsons of Abinadab, set out to accompany David and the other Israelites on this festive pilgrimage. Since the house of Abinadab had long been charged with taking care of the ark (1 Sam 7:1-2), it is not surprising that Uzzah and Ahio served as "grand marshals" of the parade by actually driving the cart carrying the ark toward Jerusalem. What is surprising, however, is what happened to Uzzah along the way.

• *Transferring the ark: a temporary delay (vv. 6-11).* The festive religious parade came to a screeching halt when Uzzah—after reaching out his hand in an effort to steady the ark, which had been shaken because of the stumbling oxen—suddenly died. We are not told how Uzzah died, but that "the anger of the LORD was kindled against Uzzah" and that "God smote him there...and he died there beside the ark" (v. 7).

This incident disturbed David so much that he cancelled the parade. He was afraid to take the ark to Jerusalem, so the ark was placed in the home of Obed-edom. This whole puzzling and mysterious episode left David frightened and angry.

On the surface, this account of Uzzah's death disturbs us, too. The death penalty seems harsh for the seemingly innocent act of keeping the ark from falling off the oxen cart. But there is much more to the story. Long ago, the Lord via Moses had given some explicit instructions regarding the transportation of the ark. Chief among these instructions was the command that human hands were *never* to touch the ark; rather, Levitical priests were to carry the ark on poles inserted through rings attached to the sides (Ex 25:13-14; 1 Chr 15:14-15).

Uzzah did not follow the Lord's instructions. He resolved to manage the ark of God his own way. The clue to Uzzah's disobedience is back in verse 3: "They [Uzzah and Ahio] carried the ark of God on a new cart." Rather than relying on God's method of ark transportation—the reverent, personal involvement of consecrated priests—Uzzah embraced the latest Philistine technology to transport the ark. As Eugene Peterson has observed, "When...Uzzah reflexively reaches out to keep the ark from sliding off, it is not an isolated act; it is Uzzah's *habit* to manage the ark, and supposedly along with it God-in-the-ark. The eventual consequence of this kind of obsessional management of God is death, whether slow or sudden. God will not be put and kept in a box.... We do not take care of God; God takes care of us" (163).

• *Transferring the ark: the journey resumes (vv. 12-16).* For three months, the ark remained in the house of Obed-edom. During this period, the "LORD blessed the household of Obed-edom and all that belonged to him" (vv. 11-12). When David heard about Obed-edom's good fortune, he interpreted this news as a signal that it was now safe and within the context of God's will to bring the ark to Jerusalem, so arrangements were quickly made, and the journey of the ark to Jerusalem resumed.

What a journey it was! The people joyfully worshiped God as the ark of the Lord was transported into the city. This time, the ark was carried by Israelite worshipers (v. 12). The people of Israel enthusiastically praised and worshiped God.

David was right in the midst of, and even leading, this joyful and unrestrained praise and worship of God! David did not just order that the ark be brought to Jerusalem; rather, he led the resumed ark procession himself. Notice David's involvement: he apparently offered a sacrificial offering to God (v. 13); he "leaped" and "danced before the LORD with all his might" (vv. 14, 16); and he apparently joined in the joyful shouting of praise to God as the ark procession edged forward, accompanied by the sound of trumpets (v. 15).

Eugene Peterson notes that the word "worship" is not found in this passage about worship. What is found is "dancing," which is used four times (vv. 5, 14, 16, 21) to describe David's worship of God. Peterson notes, "Dancing as a metaphor for worship gives the sense that our response to God takes us out of ourselves, sets us free from the plod of merely getting across the street, pulls us into a divine dance" (165). For far too long, the people of Israel under Saul had all but kept God off the dance floor of their lives. By transferring the ark to Jerusalem, David invited God to the center of Israel's dance floor. As the leader of Israel, David reminded the people to worship God—to participate in the divine dance!

Understanding

David's decision to "house" the ark of God in Jerusalem cannot be overemphasized. The people of Israel would now view Jerusalem as the "holy city"—the religious capital—of Israel. Under David, Jerusalem—not some potentially religiously divisive "northern" or "southern" city—would become the center for Israel's worship of God.

More importantly, David's decision to bring the ark out of "exile," back to the center stage of Israelite life, provided an answer to a question that must have been on the minds of many Israelites—namely, what kind of king would David be? Would he aspire to become a king like the other monarchs in the ancient Near East? Would he dare regard himself and demand that his subjects regard himself as divine? The transfer of the ark of God to Jerusalem answered this question with a resounding "no." David, early on described as a man "after God's own heart" (1 Sam 13:14), would reign as God's representative and submit his kingship to the Lord. God, not David, would be worshiped. God would be recognized as *the King*.

Here, then, is David demonstrating by his actions that he is—in the best developmental sense of the word—a wise and mature adult. David could have used his power as king to serve his own needs. For example, he could have named Hebron (where he had already established headquarters during his previous reign as king of Judah) as the new capital of Israel. However, David opted to meet the needs of all his constituents by naming the neutral Jerusalem as Israel's new capital. Moreover, David could have chosen to leave the ark on the margins of Israelite life. By transferring the ark to Jerusalem, David made a dramatic statement that God would be recognized as the real "King" of Israel. David desired to put the Lord at the center of Israelite life.

Because of his desire to give priority to God and due to his efforts in placing the needs of the Israelites ahead of his own preferences, David displayed wise and mature leadership whereby he used his gifts to become "part of the answer rather than part of the problem." The wise and mature "adult David" possessed leadership skills that worked!

What About Me?

- *God desires and deserves to be at the center of our lives.* We are not to keep God on the margins of our existence only to allow God front and center whenever we feel like it or whenever we have some crisis or need. Rather, the Lord desires to be *the King* of every facet of our living.

- *We cannot take charge of God.* We are foolish to think that we can somehow manage the Lord by "keeping God in a box," whether the "box" is one constructed of ornate wood or one formed by our own guidelines or one built by our own interpretations of how God must be! "We do not take care of God; God takes care of us" (Peterson, 163).

- *We cannot fully "explain" God.* We cannot satisfactorily explain the seemingly unfair death of Uzzah for "touching the ark" in human terms. This side of heaven, we will always have to live without the answers to some, if not many, of our "How could...?" and "Why?" questions. As humans, we really do now "know only in part"; we can often only "see in a mirror, dimly" (1 Cor 13:12). Because we are not God, we must have the faith that is necessary "to let God be God." We must be willing at times to let the Mystery stand.

- *There is a time to dance (and a time to refrain from dancing).* In other words, there is a time for festive, celebrative, and even uninhibited worship. There is a time for more reflective, quiet, and contemplative worship, too. Wise is the person who knows what time it is in this important worship area of his or her life.

- *Adulthood is far more than some chronological milestone.* Adulthood occurs when we are mature enough to serve and care for others as opposed to focusing on how others can always meet our needs and serve us. Certainly, the Lord had "adult" followers in mind when declaring, "Whoever wishes to become great among you must be your servant, and whoever wishes to be first among you must be your slave" (Mk 10:43-44). In short, God is looking for some adult servant-followers (like David of old) who are mature enough to "become part of the answer instead of part of the problem" (Claypool, 65).

Resources

A. A. Anderson, *2 Samuel*, Word Biblical Commentary, vol. 11 (Dallas: Word Books, 1989).

Leith Anderson, *Leadership That Works: Hope and Direction for Church and Parachurch Leaders in Today's Complex World* (Minneapolis: Bethany House Publishers, 1999).

Walter Brueggemann, *David's Truth in Israel's Imagination & Memory* (Philadelphia: Fortress Press, 1985).

———, *First and Second Samuel*, Interpretation: A Bible Commentary for Teaching and Preaching (Louisville: John Knox Press, 1990).

John Claypool, *Stages: The Art of Living the Expected* (Waco: Word Books, 1980).

H. J. Katzenstein, "Philistines," *The Anchor Bible Dictionary*, vol. 5 (New York: Doubleday, 1992).

J. Maxwell Miller, "David," *Mercer Dictionary of the Bible*, ed. Watson E. Mills et al. (Macon GA: Mercer University Press, 1990).

Eugene H. Peterson, *First and Second Samuel* (Louisville: Westminster John Knox Press, 1999).

Ben Philbeck Jr., "1–2 Samuel," *The Broadman Bible Commentary*, vol. 3 (Nashville: Broadman Press, 1970).

THE ADULT DAVID:
DANCING BEFORE THE LORD
2 Samuel 6:1-15

Introduction

The Bible says clearly, "There is a time to dance" (Eccl 3:4). The season of life we call adulthood is one of those times. If adolescence is a time to grow out of childhood into maturity, then adulthood is a time to enjoy that maturity, to celebrate it and to deepen it as well.

Dancing is usually associated with joy and vitality. According to the Oxford American Desk Dictionary, to dance is "to move in rhythm, to move in a lively way or with lively motion." I grew up being told that dancing is bad—an idea reflected by Michal in this story (6:16, 20). However, David suggests his dancing was a deeply spiritual and worshipful thing to do "before the LORD" (6:21).

I guess almost anything can be seen in at least two ways. This "every-coin-has-two-sides" idea is very much at the heart of this session. First, it is about the rhythm of relating between God, David, and God's people. This is a rhythm that mature adulthood was made for—to know who God is, to know who I am and why I am here, and to learn how to relate in more healthy ways to others.

Second, this session is about the recognition and celebration of both sides of the coin as a way to include all God's people in the covenant relationship. One side of this ark before which David danced points to the past and the beginnings of Israel's faith; the other side points to the future and the unification and calling of Israel. We might even view adulthood as a dance between the two sides of various coins.

I. David Brings the Ark of God

The word "ark" has multiple meanings in the Bible. Derived from the Latin, arca, which can mean "chest, box or basket," early in Scripture, the word is used of the boat Noah built and by which his family survived the flood. Then, it is used of the basket—or floating cradle—in which Moses' mother placed him. That ark saved Moses from the murderous insecurity of Pharaoh, just as Noah's ark provided salvation from the waters. Thus, the ark is a symbol of the saving ability of God as well as the presence of God.

To David the ark was a spiritual object that served to remind Israel of the formal relationship (covenant) between God and Israel. It called Israel back to the taproot of its faith and reminded them that Yahweh is the God who saves. The ark's basic meaning is that salvation (wholeness and well-being) comes from God, not from big soldiers or huge armaments, as we saw in last week's session.

The ark was "a near embodiment of God's presence" (1 Sam 4:1-9). We might even compare it to the bread and cup we use in the supper of our Lord. They are sacred symbols that God loves us. Moreover, God saves us and remains with us to sustain us and lead us into adult spiritual maturity.

II. David and Israel Growing Toward Godliness

David is now an adult, growing into the fullness of his power as king. He wanted to center Israel in the trust and worship of Yahweh, so he chose the ark, even though it had been set aside and neglected for years, as a symbol of that spiritual unity and vitality. He wanted to bring together the claims of the covenant with Yahweh plus the new idea of a monarchy centered in Jerusalem to unify Israel.

Walter Brueggemann says, "The coming of the Ark signified two things.... At the same time the narrative looks back to tribal vitality and forward to royal legitimacy.... Insofar as it looks back, it looks back to genuine religious seriousness on David's part. Insofar as it looks forward, it does so with a hint of political calculation" (*I and II Samuel*, Interpretation: A Bible Commentary for Teaching and Preaching [Louisville: John Knox Press, 1990] 249). David was coming into his own as a mature adult. Meanwhile, Israel was maturing not just as a people, a nation, or a political power, but spiritually in a way it never could have with Saul as king.

David's kingship began in a worship experience of sacrifice and obedience to God—rather than a political process (1 Sam 16:1-13). The adult David wanted to incorporate the ark as a symbol of Israel's spiritual vitality and of his leadership. This was an act of worship—and it prompted David to dance before the Lord.

We learn from our Lord that nothing is as joyful in life as following the leadership of God into the fullness of who you were made to be and what you were called to do—even though it involves pain and struggle and maybe even a cross. In the New Testament, Hebrews witnesses to this idea: "Let us lay aside every weight and the sin that clings so closely, looking to Jesus the pioneer and perfecter of our faith, who for the sake of the joy that was set before him, endured the cross, disregarding its shame, and has taken his seat at the right hand of the throne of God" (Heb 12:1-2).

III. The Strange Story of Uzzah

The ark of God is a visible, tangible reminder that our salvation is from God, not from ourselves. It reminds us that battles such as Israel vs. Pharaoh or of David vs. Goliath were won "in the name of the Lord of Hosts," not in the strength of human power and ingenuity. Salvation comes only from God.

The story of Uzzah (6:6-11) makes a valid point, although strange to us. In this episode, Uzzah reached out to steady the ark after the oxen jostled it. However, when it comes to something as sacred as salvation, God doesn't need our help. The basic truth, the truth Saul had lost sight of, is that we don't do God's work in our own strength. If we try, the work becomes ours instead of God's. We must trust God. There is no other salvation.

Furthermore, we can't take God's presence for granted. Touching the ark was like touching God. The ark could not be taken for granted, or treated with familiarity. It is not ours to use; it is God's to give: "To touch it is to impinge on God's holiness, to draw too close and presume too much.... When people are no longer awed, respectful or fearful of God's holiness, the community is at risk" (Brueggemann, *I and II Samuel*, 249).

We are not called to defend—we are called to obey and follow God. We are called to remember that God is God and we are not. To assume that we can be familiar with God is to trifle with the sacred reality that God is always and only the source of our salvation.

IV. The Dance of Mature Joy in Covenant with God

Dancing has something to do with movement, rhythm, and vitality. If we look at these three words in reverse order, *vitality* is what God gave humans when we were created in God's image. We—male and female—became a living (vital) soul (Gen 1:27). Vitality is, at its deepest level, spiritual vitality because it is a gift of God to us human beings. Vitality is what Samuel saw in young David—spiritual vitality. Now we see it in the adult David.

Rhythm is the cooperation and symmetry of living out this vitality in relationship with the God who created us. The measure, meter, tempo, and beat of the rhythm remind us of the rhythm of inhaling and exhaling the gift of breath—which gives vitality and life to our physical bodies. Remember that the word for breath in both the Old and New Testament is also the word for Spirit. The rhythm of breath is a spiritual cadence, not simply a biological one.

Movement refers to spiritual growth or progressive development. To use Paul's image, as we move in rhythm with God, we develop from infants who can only tolerate milk into adults who can handle strong meat. Hence, we grow into the fullness of all it means to be a human being and a worshiper of God. Listen to the Apostle Paul: "And so, brothers and sisters, I could not speak to you as spiritual people, but rather as people of the flesh, infants in Christ. I fed you with milk, not solid food, for you were not ready" (1 Cor 3:1-2).

Maturity, spiritual development, and growth all have more to do with this movement in rhythm with God and each other than with growth that merely gets bigger. Growth that is merely numerical, architectural, or geographic may be shallow or even cancerous growth. This kind of growth kills the spirit instead of making the spirit vital and free. In fact, in either the religious or political venues, spiritual maturity can be squelched by too much focus on power, self-interest, numbers, buildings, and land.

Saul and David provide us with an excellent picture of this contrast. Powerful Saul wanted to build a bigger kingdom. But he was selfish and secular instead of spiritually motivated. David, on the other hand, was "a man after God's own heart" (1 Sam 13:14). He wanted to lead the people into valid covenant with God and unification with each other.

V. The Ark's Home in Jerusalem

David brought the ark to Jerusalem. Solomon later placed it in the new temple he built after David's death. It continued as a spiritual symbol of God's ability to save and human ability to engage in worship, spiritual development, and service of God rather than self. The ark stayed in Solomon's temple until it was "likely destroyed when the Temple was burned by the Babylonians in 587 or 586 BC" (Lloyd R. Bailey, "Ark," *The Mercer Dictionary of the Bible*, ed. Watson E. Mills et al. [Macon GA: Mercer University Press, 1990] 63).

As we worship and follow God, we are called to live out the balances, blends, and ambiguities of the coins in our lives which indeed have two sides. Consider the six balances David struggled with:
• David is a godly man and king—David is all too human
• The kingdom is God's—the kingdom must deal with political reality
• David dances before the ark—Uzzah is struck down when he touches it
• The kingdom grows out of the taproot of faith—the kingdom must change, develop, and grow as time changes and challenges come
• Assurance that God is present—we dare not take God's presence for granted
• David humbles himself in nakedness before the Lord—David is exalted as the greatest king in Israel's history

Jesus makes the same point when he says that to be humble before God leads to being exalted by God. Michal sought to disdain David. She remained tied to her father, Saul, and to Saul's way of being king. She attacked David for making a spectacle before the people. She hated him in a way that denied his value.

Yet David's risk of worshiping God in this strange way proved to be a way of illustrating that when we exalt ourselves, we are humbled; when we humble ourselves, we are exalted by God (Mt 23:12; Lk 14:11; 18:14).

This kind of worship is not a strategy for egotistic climbing into places of power and honor. It is the way the economy of God works when we bow before God in worship and God raises us to newness of life in the power of resurrection.

Notes

Notes

3

THE MIDLIFE DAVID: FRUSTRATED AND FOOLISH

2 Samuel 11

Central Question

When are people especially susceptible to the "sin of entitlement"?

Scripture

2 Samuel 11:2-17 It happened, late one afternoon, when David rose from his couch and was walking about on the roof of the king's house, that he saw from the roof a woman bathing; the woman was very beautiful. 3 David sent someone to inquire about the woman. It was reported, "This is Bathsheba daughter of Eliam, the wife of Uriah the Hittite." 4 So David sent messengers to get her, and she came to him, and he lay with her. (Now she was purifying herself after her period.) Then she returned to her house. 5 The woman conceived; and she sent and told David, "I am pregnant." 6 So David sent word to Joab, "Send me Uriah the Hittite." And Joab sent Uriah to David. 7 When Uriah came to him, David asked how Joab and the people fared, and how the war was going. 8 Then David said to Uriah, "Go down to your house, and wash your feet." Uriah went out of the king's house, and there followed him a present from the king. 9 But Uriah slept at the entrance of the king's house with all the servants of his lord, and did not go down to his house. 10 When they told David, "Uriah did not go down to his house," David said to Uriah, "You have just come from a journey. Why did you not go down to your house?" 11 Uriah said to David, "The ark and Israel and Judah remain in booths; and my lord Joab and the servants of my lord are camping in the open field; shall I then go to my house, to eat and to drink, and to lie with my wife? As you live, and as your soul lives, I will not do such a thing." 12 Then David said to Uriah, "Remain here today also, and tomorrow I will send you back." So Uriah remained in Jerusalem that day. On the next day, 13 David invited him to eat and drink in his presence and made him drunk; and in the evening he went out to lie on his couch with the servants of his lord, but he did not go down to his house. 14 In the morning David wrote a letter to Joab, and sent it by the hand of Uriah. 15 In the letter he wrote, "Set Uriah in the forefront of the hardest fighting, and then draw back from him, so that he may be struck down and die." 16 As Joab was besieging the city, he assigned Uriah to the place where he knew there were valiant warriors. 17 The men of the city came out and fought with Joab; and some of the servants of David among the people fell. Uriah the Hittite was killed as well.

Reflecting

In his book *Men in Midlife Crisis*, pastor and writer Dr. Jim Conway describes his own midlife crisis:

> My depression had grown all through the spring, summer, and fall. By October, it had reached giant proportions.... I had literally come to the bottom of me. I was ready to chuck everything. Repeatedly I had fantasies of getting on a sailboat and sailing off to some un-known destination where no one knew me and where I carried no responsibility for anyone in my church or my family.
>
> By mid-November the depression had grown to unbelievable proportions.... On a cold, wintry night, I went for a long walk and made some decisions. I would resign as pastor of the church, write a letter...dropping my doctoral program, and write to my publishers to tell them I no longer would be writing. I would also legally turn everything over to Sally, take only our 1968 Cutlass, and start driving south. For me, it was all over. I had had it with people, with responsibility, with society, even with God, who had been such a close friend all of my adult life. He seemed now to be distant and remote, uninterested in the agony through which I was going. (11-12)

Quite a few midlife adults—both male and female—can empathize with Conway. Indeed, the so-called "midlife crisis" often results from the prolonged feeling of wanting to chuck everything and to get away from it all. Such feelings may have played a major role in the infamous David and Bathsheba affair recorded in 2 Samuel 11.

Remembering

The story of David and Bathsheba is part of a larger block of Scripture known as the Succession Narrative (2 Sam 9–20; 1 Kgs 1–2). The Succession Narrative revolves around the question, "Who should sit on the throne of my lord the king after [David]?" (1 Kgs 1:20). One of the overriding concerns of the story is how Solomon (rather than his older brothers) became David's successor.

A closer examination reveals that these Scriptures provide much more than the answer to the "Who-will-succeed-David-as-king?" question. What we have is an intimate look at the person of David during his midlife through his senior adult years—a "behind-the-scenes" view of a very public person who was idealized. David, however, is taken off the pedestal, for we see him struggle with temptations, family members, political supporters, foreign and domestic enemies, and God.

The David that we encounter in today's text could be regarded as the "midlife David." It is a time of passage from adulthood to senior adulthood.

There are no exact chronological ages at which people finds themselves in the in-between time of midlife. Midlife is learning to deal with the recognition that time is running out—that life is probably at least (if not more than) half over (Conway, 32).

Jim Conway has identified four major enemies that confront mid-lifers: (1) one's body—beginning to "feel old" and noticing the body's "aging, slowing down, and losing its youthful appeal"; (2) one's work—feeling unfulfilled and trapped by one's job is common; (3) one's family—resenting one's spouse and children, reasoning that if it were not for responsibility to the family a person could do whatever they wished; and (4) one's God—blaming God for the "time is running out" feelings. Indeed, one's midlife rebellion or crisis may actually be an attempt to "get back at God" by neglecting family, job, and other responsibilities (65-68).

False solutions to dealing with these enemies can lead to disaster. One all-too-common solution for the midlife male is to have an affair. David's affair with Bathsheba follows a pattern similar to the behavior of many contemporary midlife men (Ibid., 98-113). As David and all midlife males discover, this solution is false and disastrous.

Studying

Be forewarned: the story of David and Bathsheba includes lust, adultery, deceit, murder, and cover-ups. However, to skip over the story would be to miss a pivotal biblical story detailing how God can forgive and work through imperfect people.

The "David and Bathseba" affair is so candid in its negative portrayal of David that the writer of Chronicles chose to omit this episode when recording the history of David's reign (1 Chr 20:1-3).

• *The setting (2 Sam 11:1).* Verse 1 dates David's tryst with Bathsheba to the time of an Israelite campaign against the Ammonites. The king sent his troops to battle under the command of Joab, "but David remained at Jerusalem." We do not know why David stayed behind, which is quite pertinent since the Israelites—when lobbying God and Samuel for a king—had specifically requested a monarch to "govern us and go out before us and fight our battles" (1 Sam 8:20). Perhaps David had become too valuable to the nation to risk his life in war. Perhaps the king was now secure enough in his position to rely upon others to carry out some of his royal work. Then again, perhaps David was simply getting older and was no longer the warrior he once had been. Some writers have even speculated that David's remaining at Jerusalem could be attributed to symptoms resembling some type of midlife crisis (Conway, 99-126). Whatever the reasons for David's decision to stay at home while his troops were at war, the stage was set for one of the most scandalous and sinful scenes in the Old Testament.

• *The sin (vv. 2-5).* Following an afternoon nap, David took a late afternoon stroll. From the roof of his palace, he saw a woman bathing. She was so beautiful that David decided to act upon his lustful feelings. Perhaps the first look was unavoidable, but David sent a servant "to inquire" about the woman.

The inquiry revealed that the woman was Bathsheba, the "wife of Uriah the Hittite." David's knowledge of Bathsheba's marriage, however, did not deter David's plan to appease his desire. Verbs succinctly describe David's adulterous sin in verse 4: He sent. He took. She came. He lay. Notice that "there is no hint of caring, of affection, of love—only lust. David does not call her by name, does not even speak to her. At the end of the encounter she is only 'the woman' " (Brueggemann, *First and Second Samuel*, 273; v. 5). In his haste to satisfy his own selfish desires, David used and treated another human being as something less than human.

The most telling phrase in describing this affair is "he took her" (v. 4). Earlier in Israel's history, Samuel had warned that kings were "takers" (1 Sam 8:11-19). Unfortunately, his prophecy about David was fulfilled. As the king, David had evidently come to believe that he was somehow entitled to have whatever he wanted.

It first appeared that David got away with his adulterous sin until Bathsheba told David she was pregnant. Suddenly, the "secret" sin of the "entitled" King David was in danger of being exposed!

• *The cover-up attempt (vv. 6-13).* David initiated swift action in an attempt to cover up his sin with Bathsheba. Accustomed to getting his way, David "sent" Joab a royal order: "Send me Uriah the Hittite." Notice how the verb "send" is used three times in verse 6. David sent for Bathsheba (11:3-4). He then schemed to cover up his adulterous sin by engaging in some more kingly "sending." Joab obeyed his king's command, and Uriah was sent back to Jerusalem.

The clever David sent for Uriah under the pretense of

> Later, in 2 Samuel 12:1, the Lord's "sending" of Nathan the prophet to confront the guilty king unravels David's entire cover-up plot (Brueggemann, *David's Truth*, 56-57).

discovering how Joab and the soldiers were faring against the Ammonites. However, David's real intent was to provide Uriah with the opportunity to have sexual relations with his wife so that no one would suspect that David himself was the father of Bathsheba's child (v. 8).

Most soldiers would have gladly complied with David's directive. Uriah, however, spent the night in the palace compound. When David asked why he had not gone home, Uriah declared that it would not have been right for him to sleep at home with his wife while Joab and the troops of David were fighting for their king (v. 11). Although Uriah was a Hittite mercenary in David's army, he was still so loyal that he would not break the rules of sexual abstinence required of Hebrew soldiers consecrated for war (1 Sam 21:4-5). What a contrast with David, who broke God's commandment against adultery while the loyal Uriah was fighting for David in battle!

Disappointed, David formulated another cover-up plan. That evening, David wined and dined Uriah to the point of "making him drunk" (v. 13). Even the inebriated Uriah would not risk violating the sexual abstinence code of soldiers, though.

• *Another cover-up plot (vv. 14-25).* While Uriah slept, David finalized the second cover-up plot. The next morning, the king sent Uriah back to battle—along with sealed orders directing Joab to "set Uriah in the forefront of the hardest fighting...that he may be struck down and die" (v. 15). With Uriah dead, Bathsheba's pregnancy could be assigned to her deceased husband, and David's adulterous fling would remain a secret.

Joab wasted little time carrying out the king's deadly command. Not wishing to become a scapegoat for carrying out the king's orders, Joab covered his tracks by sending David a report about the latest

 Employing tactics that all but assured heavy casualties, Joab assigned Uriah to an extremely vulnerable and dangerous position near the wall of the Ammonite city under attack. Such "near the wall" fighting was evidently rather widely regarded as foolish military strategy (v. 21; see Judg 9:50-54). However, Joab knew that such questionable battle tactics would almost certainly guarantee Uriah's death. The result of Joab's military maneuvering is hardly surprising—Uriah was killed along with other Israelite soldiers (vv. 16-17).

fighting: "Your servant Uriah the Hittite is dead also" (vv. 19-21). Having already taken Uriah's wife, David had now taken Uriah's life. This time, the cover-up apparently worked!

• *The aftermath (vv. 26-27).* Upon hearing the news from the battlefield, Bathsheba properly grieved her husband's death. When the official mourning period was over, David sent for Bathsheba, married her, and claimed her unborn baby as his own. Notice, however, that Bathsheba is not called by her own name. The biblical writer wanted us to remember her as the "wife of Uriah." Even later, in the genealogy of Jesus recorded in Matthew—a genealogy in which other women such as Tamar, Ruth, and Mary are identified by their own names—Bathsheba is still solely regarded as the "wife of Uriah" (Mt 1:6).

Seven days was regarded as the customary time for strict mourning (Gen 50:10; 1 Sam 31:13). For a widow to remarry rather quickly after the death of her husband was probably not all that uncommon in the culture of the ancient Near East. The options for a widow who did not remarry were rather limited: return to her father's house, be supported by her children, or face the difficult prospect of trying to eek out a living without any property rights or societal protection (Gen 38:11; Ruth 1:8-9; Num 27:11).

As this chapter ends, the sinful yet unrepentant David appears to have "gotten away" with his sins. Yet there is a hint that David's calculated cover-up had not been completely successful: "But the thing that David had done displeased the LORD" (v. 27). This is the first time that God has been explicitly mentioned in the story. Did David really imagine that his life could actually be lived without involving God?

Understanding

David is not the only midlife person with a false sense of entitlement. Numerous men and women in midlife—possibly feeling that their time is running out—somehow feel entitled to fool around, shirk family and work responsibilities, and behave as if God's laws no longer apply to them. In *The Success Syndrome*, psychologist Steven Berglas notes that highly talented people sometimes suddenly fall apart when they achieve certain levels of success. Often, these "successful and talented" individuals crash and burn because they develop a false sense of entitlement and succumb to one or more of the four "A"s: *arrogance, aloneness,* destructive *adventure-seeking,* or *adultery* (Maxwell, 5).

What about you? Are you ever tempted to succumb to one or more of the four "A"s? Do you ever act as if you are somehow "entitled" to put your own self-interests before anything else or to treat someone else as an object of desire, even less than human? Do you ever use your position or your power to take something that belongs to another—a spouse, reputation, job, idea, career, life? Do you ever behave as if you are somehow exempt from obeying the Lord's commandments?

Our attempt to hide our sins also makes us more like David than we care to admit. Rather than confessing wrongdoing or owning up to our mistakes, we occasionally resort to hiding our transgressions through well-contrived and sometimes quite elaborate cover-up schemes. Even when our cover-ups succeed, we—like David—must eventually reckon with the One who sees through all cover-ups, who is displeased with our sins, and who holds us accountable for living as if we are somehow entitled to disregard God's laws.

What About Me?

• *No one—regardless of power of position—is exempt from obeying God's laws.* Adultery, murder, and lying are sinful whether one is a king, a soldier, a CEO, or an average citizen. God's laws are applicable to all. No one is entitled to live above or break them.

• *The allure of lust tempts us to use and treat other human beings as something less than human.* Succumbing to lust results in our becoming "takers"—selfishly grasping what we desire while giving little or no thought to the consequences of our "taking" on others.

• *Sin has a way of entangling and negatively impacting the lives of others.* Not only does our sin hurt us; often, innocent parties are hurt as well. Our attempts at covering up our sins tend to produce a growing web of deceit, mistrust, and trouble.

• *The Bible presents a very realistic portrayal of humans.* Biblical personalities are depicted as being prone to sin. The truth about characters like David enables us to face the truth about ourselves. We are sinners. Yet as 2 Samuel 12 demonstrates, the Lord sends "Nathans" into our lives to confront us with our sins, to remind us that we are held accountable for our wrongs, and to offer us forgiveness and grace.

• *Even when confronted with the fact that time is running out on us, we can be assured that God will never run out on us.* The Lord has promised to be with us always (Mt 28:19) and never to abandon us (Deut 31:6). God is with us during the critical and often crisis-oriented stage of midlife, just as the Lord is with us throughout all the stages of our lives.

Resources

Walter Brueggemann, *David's Truth in Israel's Imagination & Memory* (Philadelphia: Fortress Press, 1985).

———, *First and Second Samuel*, Interpretation: A Bible Commentary for Teaching and Preaching (Louisville: John Knox Press, 1990).

Jim Conway, *Men in Midlife Crisis* (Elgin IL: David C. Cook Publishing, 1983).

John C. Maxwell, *The 21 Indisputable Qualities of a Leader* (Nashville: Thomas Nelson Publishers, 1999).

DAVID IN MIDLIFE:
FRUSTRATED AND FOOLISH

2 Samuel 11

Introduction

The story of David in midlife suggests two things. First, he was frustrated because he had become self-centered and lacked valid spiritual balance. Second, he was foolish because he yielded to temptations and sin. Beyond being foolish, he became a fool! The man of integrity and valid self-confidence who, as an adolescent and young adult, trusted God tragically moves away from intimacy with God and toward selfishness, arrogance, and greed.

Despite being a great king, this move brought emptiness, complexity, and heartache to David's life; confusion, betrayal, and disaster to his family; and more warfare to the kingdom of Israel. Many genuinely fine people in our own day crash and burn in midlife. It is truly a danger zone. Even with the power of a king, David could not undo what he did. He could not stop the onslaught of his sin, which multiplied itself like a rushing tide.

I. Blessing, Fidelity, and Success

Up to the affair, David's life had centered on developing a spiritual relationship with God, growing into personal maturity, and leading Israel into being a more viable nation. Success with these endeavors brought power, prominence, and privilege to David. His life was evidence of many blessings and accomplishments. He must have felt that he had "accomplished it all."

Ask yourself: What would I do if I attained power, prominence, and privilege? What comes next? For many of us, there are two basic answers. First, one could embrace a sense of God's call, taking responsibility to serve and mean something to God's kingdom and other people. In other words, assume the attitude, *I am blessed; I will be a blessing and pass this grace on.* Or one could feel a sense of entitlement that breeds indulgence, accumulation, and greed. David did the latter.

Second Samuel 5–10 presents David as a person who had truly come into his own. Enormously powerful, he was a man of chesed (pronounced hés-id)— a man of fidelity and spiritual wholeness. He was a leader who exercised power and executive decisiveness, balanced with a valid spiritual sensitivity. Tragically, as he developed as a leader, he failed to continue developing as a person.

II. Looming Dangers of Crisis

Before that fateful spring, David had led his men into battle. Now in midlife, David felt some need to delegate to others what he used to do himself. Joab answered the call to fight the Ammonites while David stayed home in Jerusalem.

David must have been thinking: *I am the King. I have earned some pampering. I am entitled to be treated as a VIP. I don't have to live by the same rules that others do.* He was not struggling as much as he did earlier in life with great personal or kingdom challenges. He was bored and frustrated. The spiritual quest that was his as a young lad and young adult had long since moved to a back burner of his life. As our title today suggests, these frustrations led to foolishness; the foolishness led to destructive sin.

III. Moral Failure

At chapter 11, the story shifts from David's public triumph and personal well-being to his moral failure, sin, and personal pathos. His life was never the same after he "took" Bathsheba. There is no sense of intimacy and tenderness in this encounter, no words spoken between them. David sent for her, took her, and dispatched her when he was finished. The account is graphic and impersonal.

Please note that in accordance with the custom of that day, the men in this sad story had their own names: David, Joab, Uriah, Nathan—all personal names. Bathsheba's hyphenated name indicates who owned her: "Bathsheba—daughter of Eliam—

wife of Uriah the Hittite." To all the men in the story, she was no more than a piece of property to be used at will, not a person of value who deserved being treated with respect.

Interestingly, this impersonal pattern continues into Matthew's first chapter. Several women appear in the lineage of Jesus: Tamar, Rahab, Ruth, Mary, and "the wife of Uriah" (vv. 3, 5-6). As mother of one of Israel's greatest kings, she still had no personal name.

IV. The Anatomy of Sin

Old Testament scholar Walter Brueggemann said of this story of David and Bathsheba, "An abrupt transition from a life under blessing to a life under curse. It is the intrusion of sin into the life of David (and Israel) that cuts so sharply that it rivals in power the "original" act of Adam and Eve. The story is so massive and penetrating that it almost defies our capacity to interpret. Every effort fails before the subject itself, no doubt the way interpretation fails all great art" (*I and II Samuel*, Interpretation: A Bible Commentary for Teaching and Preaching [Louisville: John Knox Press, 1990] 272).

Someone may ask, *What is this sin that is so destructive to human beings? What is the comparison in Brueggemann's mind between eating the apple in the garden and violating this woman who doesn't even have her own name?* Let's look at the anatomy of sin within this story. The sin is much more grievous and damaging than eating fruit or even sexual adultery.

I grew up with the notion that "all sin is bad, but sexual sin is worse than bad." Jesus, however, seems to assess the "cold-hearted sins" as more grievous than the "warm-hearted sins" (Mt 21:31-32).

Is sexual sin the worst of sins in God's eyes? Is adultery always sexual, or is it possible to adulterate relationships in other ways—such as neglect and workaholism? Was David's worst sin sexual?

Review the laundry list of sins committed in this story, keeping in mind that this list may not be exhaustive. What others might be included?
• Lusting after power and dominance
• Lusting after a beautiful woman

- Committing sexual adultery—using another person
- Committing adultery of other relationships through deceit
- Discounting the value of the woman, treating her like a replaceable thing instead of a valuable person
- Manipulating Uriah's fidelity as though he were a thing
- Ordering Joab into complicity with the plot to cover up the sin
- Ordering a murder when the cover-up doesn't work
- Making murder look like the random fortunes of war
- Covering up the diabolical plot
- Misusing power and privilege
- Acting out a sense of entitlement rather than humility
- Lacking accountability to God or God's moral authority
- Being arrogant
- Judging self-righteously Nathan's "Rich Man"

The anatomy of sin is more than eating forbidden fruit and trifling with another's property. Sin is more than foolishness and folly. Sin is a metastasizing cancer of selfishness that eats away at the integrity of one's soul. It adulterates (waters down, corrupts the quality of) all relationships—with God, self, and others.

Let me invite you to ponder a few comparisons between David and Uriah. David was an enormously blessed shepherd boy, son of a poor, less than noteworthy citizen, who became powerful and prominent as king of Israel. Uriah must have considered himself equally fortunate. He was a foreigner, not a son of Israel's faith, not a son of anyone rich or important. Yet he served the king faithfully and "possessed" a strikingly beautiful wife.

David, on the other hand, "had it all" by middle age, but he was still trying to fill something empty inside of himself. Uriah had very little materially, but it seemed to be enough. He did not have a vacuum inside himself that pressed him to acquire more, even to the extent of adultery, murder, and a self-righteous cover-up.

When we talk about sin, it is necessary to distinguish between fruit and root. Sin is wanting to be God instead of trusting God to be God. Sin—with Adam and Eve, with King David, or with you and me—is taking matters into our own hands and seeking to control them to our own advantage. Sin is not trusting God and the grace of God for our well-being. What David set in motion "was evil in the sight of Yahweh" (11:27). However, the sin was in his heart before it became a series of acts. Sin is more root than fruit.

V. Confrontation, Forgiveness, and Redemption

No matter how righteous or spiritually prominent someone is, we are all frighteningly vulnerable to the evil that lurks within our deepest selves: "All have sinned and continue to fall short of the glory of God" (Rom 3:23).

I've seen it happen: someone takes a job in good faith and then uses both the job and the people involved for his own purposes more than for serving the boss or the cause. Having agreed to serve, we become self-serving and egocentric. We try to use our position and whatever power is ours to make things go our way and deliver what we want—often at the expense of other people. We do not love God with all our heart, mind, strength and soul, and our neighbor as our self (Lk 10:25-28). We want what we want when we want it; moreover, we are tempted to take it if we can. Then, we cover up the evil we have done lest someone suspects.

This darkness makes vulnerable every human being—kings and presidents, common laborers and middle management. We are all tempted to use position to exploit rather than to serve what Paul called "the common good" (1 Cor 12:7). Even the man after God's own heart, was vulnerable to such sin and enormous evil.

Enter the prophet Nathan (2 Sam 12). His ingenious story about the rich man taking the one precious lamb from the poor man to serve for dinner incensed David! *How dare he take that poor man's pet lamb! That man deserves to die because of what he did and because he had no pity!* (12:6).

Nathan confronted David and *his* lack of pity (12:7). David, to his eternal credit, admitted his sin (12:13). Nathan announced the forgiveness of God upon the repentant king (12:13).

However, even the king could not undo such destructive damage. Even God's forgiveness could not bring Uriah back and restore the heartbreaking damage of the wake of destruction David's selfishness began. The king could not alter moral authority and spiritual reality. Even if the deeds had gone undiscovered, the soul of David would have been adulterated.

But David was capable of honestly confessing his sin and of receiving the grace of God's forgiveness. One of the foundational truths of God is this: *Nothing* is so grievously sinful that God cannot and will not forgive. *Nothing* can make God stop loving us. God redeems us in Jesus, then energizes and accompanies us in the power of the Spirit. God leads us to repentance, spiritual growth, and ministry to others when we are willing to bow in humble adoration and rise up to be God's servant-partners in investment for the kingdom.

Thanks be to God: Frustration and foolishness can be forgiven.

Notes

Notes

4

THE SENIOR ADULT DAVID: PASSING ON A LEGACY

1 Kings 1:1–2:12

Central Question

What legacy will you pass on to others?

Scripture

1 Kings 1:1, 5-21, 29-31, 38-48; 2:1-3, 10-12 King David was old and advanced in years; and although they covered him with clothes, he could not get warm.... 5 Now Adonijah son of Haggith exalted himself, saying, "I will be king"; he prepared for himself chariots and horsemen, and fifty men to run before him. 6 His father had never at any time displeased him by asking, "Why have you done thus and so?" He was also a very handsome man, and he was born next after Absalom. 7 He conferred with Joab son of Zeruiah and with the priest Abiathar, and they supported Adonijah. 8 But the priest Zadok, and Benaiah son of Jehoiada, and the prophet Nathan, and Shimei, and Rei, and David's own warriors did not side with Adonijah. 9 Adonijah sacrificed sheep, oxen, and fatted cattle by the stone Zoheleth, which is beside En-rogel, and he invited all his brothers, the king's sons, and all the royal officials of Judah, 10 but he did not invite the prophet Nathan or Benaiah or the warriors or his brother Solomon. 11 Then Nathan said to Bathsheba, Solomon's mother, "Have you not heard that Adonijah son of Haggith has become king and our lord David does not know it? 12 Now therefore come, let me give you advice, so that you may save your own life and the life of your son Solomon. 13 Go in at once to King David, and say to him, 'Did you not, my lord the king, swear to your servant, saying: Your son Solomon shall succeed me as king, and he shall sit on my throne? Why then is Adonijah king?' 14 Then while you are still there speaking with the king, I will come in after you and confirm your words." 15 So Bathsheba went to the king in his room. The king was very old; Abishag the Shunammite was attending the king. 16 Bathsheba bowed and did obeisance to the king, and the king said, "What do you wish?" 17 She said to him, "My lord, you swore to your servant by the LORD your God, saying: Your son Solomon shall succeed me as king, and he shall sit on my throne. 18 But now suddenly Adonijah has become king, though you, my lord the king, do not know it. 19 He has sacrificed oxen, fatted cattle, and sheep in abundance, and has invited all the children of the king, the priest Abiathar, and Joab the commander of the army; but your servant Solomon he has not invited. 20 But you, my lord the king—the eyes of all Israel are on you to tell them who shall sit on the throne of my lord the king after him. 21 Otherwise it will come to pass, when my lord the king sleeps with his ancestors, that my son Solomon and I will be counted offenders."... 29 The king swore, saying, "As the LORD lives, who has saved my life from every adversity, 30 as I swore to you by the LORD, the God of Israel, 'Your son Solomon shall succeed me as king, and he shall sit on my throne in my place,' so will I do this day." 31 Then Bathsheba bowed with her face to the ground, and did obeisance to the king, and said, "May my lord King David live forever!"... 38 So the priest Zadok, the prophet Nathan, and Benaiah son of Jehoiada, and the Cherethites and the Pelethites, went down and had Solomon ride on King David's mule, and led him to Gihon. 39 There the priest Zadok took the horn of oil from the tent and anointed Solomon. Then they blew the trumpet, and all the people said, "Long live King Solomon!" 40 And all the people went up following him, playing on pipes and rejoicing with great joy, so that the earth quaked at their noise. 41 Adonijah and all the guests who were with him heard it as they finished feasting. When Joab heard the sound of the trumpet, he said, "Why is the city in an uproar?" 42 While he was still speaking, Jonathan son of the priest Abiathar arrived. Adonijah said, "Come in, for you are a worthy man and surely you bring good news." 43 Jonathan answered Adonijah, "No, for our lord King David has made Solomon king; 44 the king has sent with him the priest Zadok, the prophet Nathan, and Benaiah son of Jehoiada, and the Cherethites and the Pelethites; and they had him ride on the king's mule; 45 the priest Zadok and the prophet Nathan have anointed him king at Gihon; and they have gone up from there rejoicing, so that the city is in an uproar. This is the noise that you heard. 46 Solomon now sits on the royal throne. 47 Moreover the king's servants came to congratulate our lord King David, saying, 'May God make the name of Solomon more famous than yours, and make his throne greater than your throne.' The king bowed in worship on the bed 48 and went on to pray thus, 'Blessed be the LORD, the God of Israel, who today has granted one of my offspring to sit on my throne and permitted me to witness it.' " 2:1 When David's time to die drew near, he charged his son Solomon, saying: 2 "I am about to go the way of all the earth. Be strong, be courageous, 3 and keep the charge of the LORD your God, walking in his ways and keeping his statutes, his commandments, his ordinances, and his testimonies, as it is written in the law of Moses, so that you may prosper in all that you do and wherever you turn."... 10 Then David slept with his ancestors, and was buried in the city of David. 11 The time that David reigned over Israel was forty years; he reigned seven years in Hebron, and thirty-three years in Jerusalem. 12 So Solomon sat on the throne of his father David; and his kingdom was firmly established.

Reflecting

In one section of *The 7 Habits of Highly Effective People*, Stephen Covey invites the reader to imagine attending the funeral of a loved one. Covey skillfully leads the reader through each stage of this activity—driving to the funeral chapel, parking the car, walking inside the building, noticing the flowers, seeing the faces of family members and friends, and feeling the mixed emotions of sorrow and gratitude emanating from those in attendance. As the reader walks down to view the body of the deceased, "you suddenly come face to face with yourself. This is your funeral, three years from today" (96).

The program for "your" funeral indicates that there will be four speakers: a family member, a close friend, someone from your work or profession, and an individual from your church. Covey then asks the reader what he or she would want each of these speakers to say. How would the reader want to be remembered? What legacy would the reader leave behind (Ibid., 96-97)?

Covey's exercise illustrates what he calls "beginning with the end in mind." Who among us could not profit from evaluating how we are living? Who among us could not stand to be more intentional about getting our priorities straight? Who among us does not need to evaluate from time to time how we want to be remembered?

Remembering

The material recorded in 1 Kings 1-2 is the conclusion to the Succession Narrative (2 Sam 9-20; 1 Kgs 1-2). Recall that the Succession Narrative is a cohesive literary unit concerned with the question, "Who should sit on the throne after [David]?"

We meet "the senior adult David" in our text for today. Indeed, the David of 1 Kings 1-2 has entered into what John Claypool terms "the evening of life." Although in the last stage of his earthly journey, David's life had not become any less complicated or stressful. Even while trying to cope with a deteriorating body, David felt compelled to focus on his legacy. As he was "setting his affairs in order," the issue of his successor became an overriding concern not only for David, but for the entire nation of Israel as well.

Studying

• The elderly King David (1 Kgs 1:1-4). These verses describe the deteriorating physical condition of David (v. 1). The king "could not get warm." The time for naming a new king was rapidly approaching.
• Adonijah "claims" the throne (vv. 5-10). As the oldest living son of David (2 Sam 3:2-4), Adonijah was not alone in his expectation that he should be the next king. Both Joab, the commander of

David's army, and Abiathar, a priest whom David had consulted, believed that Adonijah should be David's successor (v. 7). Besides, Adonijah was "a very handsome man" (v. 6). Furthermore, Adonijah had already amassed chariots, horsemen, and a contingent of other supporters (v. 5). He was acting like a king!

Not everyone, however, was convinced that Adonijah should be king. Among those opposing Adonijah's kingship were Zadok, the priest closely associated with the ark of the covenant; Benaiah, the commander of the foreign mercenaries who formed a personal body guard for David; Nathan the prophet; and warriors Shimei and Rei. The listing of this opposition party in verse 8 alerts the reader to the fragile nature of Adonijah's claim to kingship.

Much like his brother Absalom had done at Hebron (2 Sam 15:7-12), Adonijah arranged to be proclaimed king at a family feast (vv. 9-10). All of David's sons, except Solomon, were invited. Also missing from the guest list were Benaiah, Nathan, Shimei, and Rei. The omission of these powerful figures indicates Adonijah's awareness of those who desired Solomon to succeed David on the throne.

• *The counterplot of Nathan and Bathsheba (1 Kgs 1:11-31).* Nathan engineered a plan to have Solomon proclaimed king. The prophet enlisted Bathsheba's help by advising her: (1) to inform David that Adonijah proclaimed himself king; and (2) to remind David that he had previously sworn that Solomon would succeed him on the throne (a promise evidently made to Bathsheba but not recorded in any other text).

Bathsheba willingly subscribed to Nathan's plan by carrying out his instructions (vv. 15-21). She also pressured David: "The eyes of all Israel are on you to tell them who shall sit on the throne of my lord the king after him" (v. 20). Nathan, according to plan, arrived at the "meeting" and confirmed Bathsheba's words (vv. 22-26). The crafty prophet added his own form of pressure to the need for David to make a "succession" decision. Inferring that the king might no longer be in complete control of key political matters, Nathan dared to ask David why "you have not let your servants know who should sit on the throne of my lord the king after him?" (v. 27).

Nathan's plan succeeded in motivating David to take action. The king swore "under oath" that Solomon "shall succeed me as king, and he shall sit on my throne in my place" (vv. 29-30).

Since Nathan had previously reprimanded David for his adultery with Bathsheba, one might find the prophet's alliance with Bathsheba somewhat strange. When Bathsheba gave birth to Solomon, however, Nathan had also delivered a message from God that the child would be called Jedidiah, meaning "because of the Lord" or "beloved of the Lord" (2 Sam 12:25). Perhaps Nathan perceived that Solomon's eventual accession to the throne was the result of divine initiative.

Just as Nathan had once held David morally accountable by confronting him with his sins with Bathsheba and Uriah (2 Sam 12), the prophet now held David vocationally accountable by confronting him with his responsibility to name his successor.

• *Solomon is anointed king (vv. 32-40).* David commanded that Solomon be anointed and enthroned as king immediately (vv. 29-30). The "pro-Solomon party" participated in the cere-

Since David was still alive, the anointing of Solomon at this juncture meant that Solomon was technically co-regent with David and would become sole ruler upon David's death (Smothers, 305).

mony. David's decision to have Solomon ride to the coronation on the king's "own mule" (v. 33) was a public signal that Solomon, not Adonijah, was the one designated by David to be his successor.

• *Adonijah panics (vv. 41-50).* Adonijah and his supporters were still celebrating Adonijah's unauthorized "claim" to the throne when the blast of the trumpet at Solomon's coronation interrupted their festivities. A messenger arrived to announce that Solomon, in accordance with the commands of David, had been anointed as Israel's king. Adonijah realized that he would be regarded as a threat to the stability of Solomon's kingship (vv. 49-50; Ex 21:12-14; 1 Kgs 2:28).

• *The reaction of Solomon (vv. 51-53).* Solomon's reaction to Adonijah's plea for mercy was uncharacteristically gracious. While sparing Adonijah's life, Solomon was not so naïve as to take an oath stipulating that he would never seek to kill his rival

half-brother. Instead, Solomon wisely issued a conditional pardon that assured protection from the king as long as Adonijah refrained from wickedness.

Later distrustful actions by Adonijah would necessitate a future decision by Solomon to have Adonijah killed (2 Kgs 2:13-25).

• *The last words of David (1 Kgs 2:1-9).* As the time of David's death "drew near," he gave final words of counsel to Solomon. These parting bits of fatherly advice actually fall into two distinct categories: admonition (vv. 2-4) and advice (vv. 5-9).

David's religious admonition was a charge for Solomon to follow God faithfully by "walking in his ways and keeping his statutes, his commandments, his ordinances, and his testimonies, as it is written in the law of Moses" (v. 3). Such religious advice would have had more of a positive impact on Solomon if David had been more consistent in "practicing what he preached." Still, the dying David encouraged Solomon to remember the Lord as he served Israel. Also, David reminded Solomon that faithfulness to God's commandments was a prerequisite for keeping a descendant of David on the throne (v. 4).

Even on his deathbed, though, David was still "David." Consider that the second half of David's last words take on a more human, politically pragmatic tone (vv. 5-9). Specifically, David instructed Solomon to do three things. First, he told Solomon to eliminate Joab (vv. 5-6). Although Joab had often been loyal to David, he had also disregarded David's orders (2 Sam 3:27; 18:9-15; 20:10). Joab's recent alliance with Adonijah made him a threat to Solomon's reign. Consequently, the need for Joab's eradication was critical. Solomon would waste little time carrying out this deathbed command of his father (2 Kgs 2:28-35).

The second element of David's pragmatic instruction called for Solomon to "deal loyally" with the descendants of Barzillai, a Gileadite who had been helpful to David when the king was fleeing from Absalom (2 Sam 17:27-29; 19:31-40). David did not want his supporters to be forgotten or mistreated.

David's third piece of advice concerned Shimei, the Benjaminite who had thrown stones at David, called him a murderer, and cursed him (2 Sam 16:5-9). David later forgave Shimei and swore that he would not kill him (2 Sam 19:23). However, David did not forget those who opposed him. His oath did not prevent David from instructing Solomon to take care of this matter. Besides, Shimei's continued loyalty to the house of Saul (2 Sam 16:8) might have proven troublesome to Solomon's administration. Shortly after David's death, Solomon found cause to have Shimei killed (1 Kgs 2:39-46).

David's life ended much like it was lived—as an ambivalent mixture of good (vv. 2-4) and evil (vv. 5-9). The David who seemed so close to God and who in his final words advised Solomon to walk in God's ways (v. 3) is the same David who commanded Solomon to seek revenge on his enemies (vv. 5-6, 8-9). This almost simultaneous *saint* and *sinner* David became the model by which all future Israelite kings would be judged. This *spiritual* and *worldly* David was used by God to unite and to lead Israel during a very politically turbulent time. This *faithful* yet *rebellious* David provides us with great hope. If God could forgive this David, surely we can also repent and receive divine forgiveness. If the Lord chose to work through the life of this David, surely God can choose to work through us!

> How would you describe the mix of worldly and spiritual, saint and sinner, in your own life?

• *The death of David (vv. 10-12).* David's death is recorded according to a formula used throughout 1–2 Kings to document the deaths of succeeding Israelite and Judean kings (see 1 Kgs 11:41-43; 14:19-20, 29-31). After years of domestic and political struggles, David's reign was passed to Solomon, who "sat upon the throne of David his father; and his kingdom was firmly established" (v. 12). The question of the Succession Narrative—the question of "who shall sit on the throne" of David—had finally been answered.

Understanding

We do not have to be senior adults to connect with the David of 1 Kings 1–2. In truth, we can connect with the senior adult David whenever we give serious consideration to our legacy. This may occur when our parents or other family members reach senior adulthood. It may happen when we make a will. It may transpire when an illness, an unexpected tragedy, a funeral, or some other crisis reminds us of our own mortality. This connection may even occur on those rare occasions when we slow down long enough from racing through life to seriously evaluate and reflect upon what we are really doing with our lives. Such reflective and evaluative times may motivate us to start setting our affairs in order now rather than waiting until some future time.

During such times of evaluation and reflection, we might profit by asking ourselves some hard questions:
(1) How do I want to be remembered?
(2) What would I like the eulogy at my funeral to declare?
(3) What am I doing with the gift of my life that will make a positive difference one year from now? Ten years from now? Twenty-five years from now? One hundred years from now?
(4) If I could live the last year of my life over again, what would I change and why?
(5) Due to the way that I am currently approaching life, what am I missing about life that I may live to regret?
(6) Is God pleased—will the Lord be pleased—with the way I am using the gift of my life?

If David's story challenges and inspires us to make the "setting of our affairs in order" a priority, then we will have made a most valuable connection with the senior adult David.

What About Me?

• *Passing on a legacy—though vitally important—is neither always easy nor void of struggle.* Passing on a worthy legacy calls for good decision-making skills, the ability to cope with conflict, the perseverance to work through tough times, and a concerted and continuing effort to use wisely the time God grants us in this life.

• *Life is a mixture of good and evil—of joy and sorrow.* Remembering this truth can assist us in keeping matters in perspective, especially during those "bad times" when we wonder if God really is in control. David's story affirms that even during times characterized by sin, God is still at work. This divine working succeeded in fashioning some good out of an extremely fractured domestic and political situation—a "Solomon" emerged to provide a much-needed period of stability.

• *God still does the unexpected.* Few people of David's day expected Solomon to be king. Our surprising God often chooses to work in unexpected ways and through unexpected people.

• *The passing on of a worthy legacy is a lifelong process.* We should not wait until the "evening of life" before we give serious consideration to the way we want to be remembered. Indeed, in a sense, we are preparing for our "final days" and formulating our legacies by the way we choose to live each stage of our lives. "So teach us to count our days that we may gain a wise heart" (Ps 90:12)—that we may leave behind and pass on to others a worthy legacy.

• *Senior adulthood is part of God's design for the human race.* Just as the Lord is with us when we are born into this world, so is the Lord with us as we exit our earthly pilgrimage. Indeed, nothing—not even senior adulthood or death—can ever separate God's followers from the Lord's love (Rom 8:37-39).

Resources

John Claypool, *Stages: The Art of Living the Expected* (Waco: Word Books, 1980).

Stephen R. Covey, *The 7 Habits of Highly Effective People* (New York: Simon & Schuster, 1989).

John Gray, *I & II Kings*, 2d ed., rev., The Old Testament Library (Philadelphia: Westminster Press, 1970).

Thomas G. Smothers, "First and Second Kings," *Mercer Commentary on the Bible*, ed. Watson E. Mills et al. (Macon GA: Mercer University Press, 1995).

THE SENIOR ADULT DAVID: PASSING ON A LEGACY

1 Kings 1:1–2:12

Introduction

One of my most effective deacons often said, "We are when we are older what we were when we were younger—only more so." This sentence rings true for me as I have observed growth (or the lack of it) in both myself and others. It is true positively and negatively.

I am older now than David was at the time of his death. I am a child, husband, father, grandfather, friend, and pastor. I have accepted that I am in the evening of my life. I am finding these years to be, as I once heard Gordon Cosby remark, both "the best and the most difficult" of all my stages of living.

How glad I am for the privilege of studying the Scripture about David's life, as well as how we may commit ourselves to keep growing *all* our lives, in all the areas of challenge God gives us!

As David did, I have committed my own self-serving sins. I have confessed these sins and been forgiven as David was. I still have a long way to go toward God's wholeness. I am grateful that I have learned to balance my growth in all the areas of challenge. I am grateful that I am aware of the necessity of serious and joyful commitment to keep growing as I age.

I have tried not to frame my retirement as "quitting" my vocation and work. I want to keep doing what I love to do in God's kingdom, only with fewer deadlines, pressures, and crises and more freedom to just "be." What a joy to be facing some new challenges of growth in my senior years.

I. Two Key Concepts

Let me recommend learning two crucially important phrases we need to know as we move toward our senior years—"spiritual development and concomitant growth." Would that David had learned these and incorporated them into his life before he reached the crises of middle age!

Spiritual development is the growth and well-being of one's soul. From a biblical viewpoint, one's soul is not "something you have"; rather, it is "someone you are." Our soul is not, as the ancient Greeks thought, a spiritual portion of a human that dwells on the inside of our bodies. Our soul is our whole being—mind, heart, and strength. Your soul is you!

Concomitant growth is a valid balance of continuing to grow in three major areas of life and commitment: (1) relationship with self, (2) relationship with family and friends, plus (3) our vocation and work. From a Christian point of view, to grow in a "concomitant" way is to grow in a balanced or blended way—not just in one or two ways—under God in all three areas of life.

We might visualize these concepts as triangles. To consider your spiritual development, visualize a triangle. Put "God" at the top of the triangle. God is Creator and Lord. The main thing in spiritual growth is to worship, adore, and follow God as Lord and leader.

At the bottom left of the triangle, put "Self." Then put "Others" on the right. Note Luke 10:25-28: "You shall love the Lord your God with all your heart, and with all your soul, and with all your strength, and with all your mind; and your neighbor as your self."

Loving self grows out of accepting how valuable you are to God. When we love God and love self we learn that God loves us and gives us value. Then, we are better equipped to love our neighbors as we love God and ourselves.

With concomitant growth, visualize a triangle with "Self" at the top, "Family and Friends" at the bottom left, and "Vocation" at the bottom right. Putting self at the top signifies that you are a uniquely gifted creation of God. Your major assignment in life is to discover and become the person God created you to be. There is no one else who has your exact assignment of relating to others and doing a valid vocation with your life for God.

Many of us make precisely the same mistake David made. In the early stages of life we can be so focused on vocation that we give less emphasis to who we will become. We spend all our energy in the morning of life preparing for how we will earn a living. We tend to neglect who we are becoming and how we will relate in healthy ways to God and the people with whom we share our lives.

To sharpen this picture, let's look at David's last days and then at how we may cooperate with God to balance our investment of our own unique gifts in the three major areas of our lives.

II. David Passes On His Legacy

David is old and cold (1 Kgs 1:1). However, David's problem was more than lack of physical warmth. David also was experiencing a loss of power. In the ancient world, the political power of a leader was basically equated with potency. Physical vigor and political effectiveness were synonymous. The king had to keep up appearances or he would become more vulnerable.

Enter Abishag (1:2-4). Her commission was to keep the king warm, but she was a caretaker, servant, and nurse. She also was there to leave the impression that the aging monarch was still vigorous and capable of leading the kingdom. He had no sexual relations with her, but few people knew that. Yet the inner circle of the king's court was all too aware that David's strength was waning. Seventy was a long time to live in those days. His depleting strength created a political vacuum.

Enter Adonijah (1:5ff), a favored child, the oldest of David's living sons. He was ambitious and self-serving, so he "exalted himself" (1:5) by assembling the ancient equivalent of an impressive motorcade to show his prowess and power. He jumped ahead of the will of David and the will of God to set himself up as David's successor. He arranged the pomp and circumstance that usually accompanies leaders, complete with an inaugural sacrifice and feast, to make abundantly clear that he was the new king (1:9-10).

Enter Nathan (1:11). Nathan had a fierce investment in the spiritual well-being of the kingdom. He knew that leadership was not just about politics and military might. He wanted a spiritual succession to Israel's throne. He had a canny sense for addressing sticky situations (remember his confrontation of David in last week's session?). So Nathan approached David's favorite wife, Bathsheba, the mother of Solomon—a wise and more mature prospect for kingship—and they hatched a plan to address the potential disaster of Adonijah becoming king by self-appointment.

David wanted Solomon to succeed him. David knew that his limitations were increasing, so he voluntarily relinquished the throne (1:47-48) to Solomon. Thus, Solomon ascended the throne by the will of David and the will of God.

The fact that some unworthy human motives and plots enabled David's will and God's sounds strange to our ears. However, God often takes what is less than pure, or even manipulative, and turns it into good for God's children.

Look at the cross and resurrection as the ultimate example that God brings good out of evil (Acts 4:27-28). Furthermore, consider similar occasions with: Joseph (Gen 50:20); Ruth and Boaz (Ruth 4:13-14); David and Bathsheba (2 Sam 12:24-25); and Absalom's insurrection (2 Sam 17:14).

David lived three score and ten years and, amid attempted coups for his throne, was able to rise to the occasion at the end of his illustrious life and pass his legacy on to Solomon. For Solomon, that legacy was a spiritual, worship-oriented, service-oriented reign.

David's story—of faith, obedience, worship, sin, forgiveness, and restoration of fellowship with God—teaches us that both spiritual and concomitant growth will help us navigate the treacherous waters of living in an unbalanced, self-oriented world—that is, if we are willing to learn from David's lack of balance and sin.

III. Senior Years: Ego-Integrity or Despair?

"What we will be at the end we are now becoming—whatever our age" (John Claypool, *The Saga of Life: Living Gracefully through the*

Stages [New Orleans: Insight Press, 2003] 83). Building on a solid foundation and with quality materials is a must. However, when we invest godly values and valid priorities as we move through our stages of life, we harvest what Erik Erikson calls "ego-integrity" in old age. When we ignore values and balances, we harvest "despair."

John Claypool said: "This time of life represents 'new ground' and poses a full set of brand new growth challenges. However, the other side of the coin is that we are preparing all through our lives for a time of agedness, whether we realize that fact or not" (Ibid.).

As a young pastor I am grateful to have found godly mentors. I suggest you do as well and as you age, learn to be a godly mentor to others. Erikson calls this task "generativity." He suggests that it should be operative during midlife so as to avoid what he calls stagnation, self-absorption and, despair (Eric Erikson, *Childhood and Society* [New York: W. W. Norton, 1950].

Generativity is the ability to look outside oneself and prepare for the next generation. If this stage of life is well done, it naturally leads to the next and final stage of ego-integrity—"coming to accept one's whole life and reflecting on it in a positive manner." Ego-integrity means fully accepting oneself and coming to terms with one's approaching death. The inability to do this will result in fear death rather than seeing it as an opening door to a new stage of life with God (Claypool, *The Saga of Life*, 83).

When my ninety-four-year-old father was facing death, he kept saying to anyone who wanted to prolong his life artificially, "You don't understand. I don't want you to just keep me here. That sounds more like existence than life. I'm ready to move on to the next thing." His trust in God was profound. He had come to know himself, embrace his past, and look forward to "the next thing," as he put it. He had learned that every exit is a new entrance.

Conclusion

After spending a month studying David, let me sum up his significance for Israel, as well as for us.

- David was the first and greatest king of Israel's united kingdom. He and Moses are the Old Testament models of leaders to this day.
- David, together with Moses, was the founder of Israel's worship. He was the author of Israel's liturgy, and the architect of Israel's Temple—though Solomon actually built it.
- David remains always in the background...the image of what once was and the ideal expression of what might be again.

As a spiritual leader, David was all of this. He began his service chosen by God through Samuel and ended it by passing God's anointing on to Solomon. As a person, David was exemplary in so many ways. Although he sinned grievously and disastrously, he owned his sins, repented, and was forgiven by God.

David made tragic mistakes from which we can learn. He ignored the opportunity to balance his life in the key areas of self-development and family relationships—putting most of his energy into vocation and accomplishment. Hopefully, you and I will learn from his poor priorities and unbalanced choices so as to let God help us balance our lives in a more redemptive manner.

Notes

Notes

nextsunday
STUDIES

1 Peter
Keep Hope Alive

This study of First Peter focuses on keeping hope alive in the face of pressures and circumstances that could possibly extinguish it completely, or worse, turn authentic faith into a pale replica of the real thing.

Advent Virtues

The phrase "holiday rush" is not an exaggeration. The frantic pace required to purchase gifts, bake holiday foods, and attend Christmas parties, plays, and performances takes its toll; we arrive at Christmas Day exhausted. Within the context of December busyness, the ancient Christian season of Advent takes on new meaning and acquires renewed importance. May God instill the virtues of *hope*, *peace*, *joy*, *love*, and *faith* in each of us this Advent.

Apocalyptic Literature

This study examines five apocalyptic texts in the Bible—from Zechariah, Daniel, Matthew, and Revelation. With each new year bringing a new prediction of impending doom, it is always a perfect time to get the story straight. Apocalyptic literature does not address the future. It addresses our present.

Approaching a Missional Mindset

The World isn't the same as it once was. We must be the church in a new place, in unimagined ways, and with a wider range of people. Engage your small group with the radical and refreshing challenge of developing a "missional lifestyle."

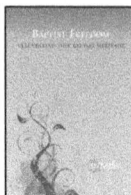

Baptist Freedom
Celebrating Our Baptist Heritage
What makes a Baptist a Baptist? Of course, the ultimate answer is simple: membership in a local Baptist church. But there are all kinds of Baptist churches! What are the spiritual and theological marks of a Baptist? What is the shape and the feel of Baptist Christianity?

The Bible and the Arts
God has used artistic expression throughout the centuries to convey truth, offer blessing, and urge believers to deeper faithfulness. In modern life, artistic expression flourishes, from movies to books to music to paintings to photographs. Sometimes artists are intentional about trying to portray God's truths. Other times, perhaps God is working even when the artist is unaware of it. As believers, we may hear and see God at work in many art forms.

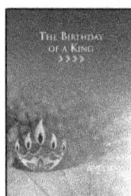

The Birthday of a King
The first four lessons in this unit draw inspiration from a traditional interpretation of the Advent candles as the Prophets' Candle, the Bethlehem Candle, the Shepherds' Candle, and the Angels' Candle. The final lesson, which occurs after Advent, celebrates the theological meaning of Jesus' birth as described in the prologue to John's Gospel.

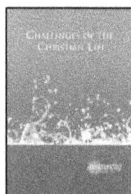

Challenges of the Christian Life
The way of the cross is difficult, and taking Jesus seriously means looking honestly at how we fall short of God's best hopes for us and seeing how much we need God's grace. For all of us there are times when we need to remember that Christ is our saving grace and recommit ourselves to the journey of faith, rediscovering, again and again, the life-giving purpose described in the book of Ephesians.

Christ Is Born!
Even in the midst of difficult circumstances, Advent is a time when we can find hope. Much like today, people in the 1st century church faced struggles. Examining the Gospel of Matthew, lessons include "Waiting for Christ," "Preparing for Christ," "Expecting Christ," "Announcing Christ," and "The Arrival of Christ."

Christians and Hunger

These sessions challenge us to apply gospel lenses and holy imagination to what literally gives us energy to live: food. With God's grace, we have the opportunity to imagine communities where tables are large and all are fed.

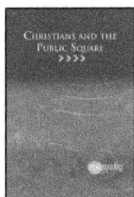

Christians and the Public Square

Politics and faith are tricky areas for Christians to negotiate. The First Amendment to the Constitution guarantees religious freedom for all Americans. As Christians who are also citizens, questions abound: How do we distinguish between faithful and unfaithful forms of civic engagement? How do we give Caesar his due while giving our all to God?

Christmas in Mark

In the early chapters of Mark, we will encounter a Christmas story. This story, however, will not be quite like the one told by other Gospel writers, but it will resonate with the reality of your life. Mark doesn't deny the beauty or reality of the nativity; however, he seems to believe that Christmas begins—the gospel begins— when Christ intrudes upon the hard realities of life.

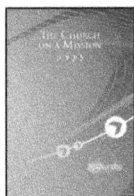

The Church on a Mission

What does it mean to be a church on a mission? The lesson of Acts 1:8 is that we must simultaneously carry out Christ's mandate at home, in our region, in places that have been our blind spots, and around the world.

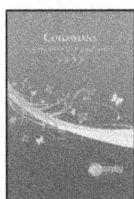

Colossians
Living the Faith Faithfully

Paul's letter to the Colossians begins with a high-minded philosophical defense of the faith, but concludes with a collection of extremely practical advice for living by faith. This study addresses the questions many Christians face today, helping them apply Paul's practical advice in their own lives.

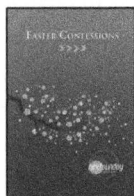

Easter Confessions

Easter confession is often found on many different lips in the Gospel of John. When we listen carefully, those ancient confessions still echo into this new millennium.

Embracing the Word of God

We live during a time of transition in Christian history. Basic assumptions about the truth of the Christian faith are being questioned, not only by nonbelievers, but by Christians themselves. First John offers a starting point for understanding of what it means to "be" Christian.

Esther: A Woman of Discretion and Valor

The book of Esther is not a record of historical facts as such. Rather, it is a magnificent narrative that refuses to interpret life as being driven by coincidence or happenstance. In the otherwise unknown characters of Esther, Haman, and Mordecai, we trace the movement of the divine hand as God collaborates with God's risk-taking people to rescue them from the hand of their enemies.

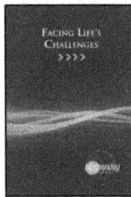

Facing Life's Challenges

This study explores four significant challenges common to most persons of faith: the challenge of new light, the challenge of time's limit, the challenge of living with mystery, and the challenge of authentic spirituality. Although these issues are neither simple nor easy to ponder, this study effectively leads us in confronting these challenges.

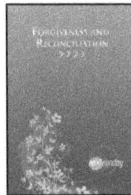

Forgiveness and Reconciliation

Forgiveness is a central issue in our capacity to remain redemptively connected to those relationships we prize. Restoring broken or interrupted relationships is a primary issue for all of us, and managing forgiveness is crucial to the possibility of experiencing reconciliation. Several dimensions of forgiveness affect our lives in significant ways. In this study, we attempt to address a few of those important issues.

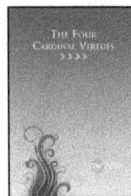

The Four Cardinal Virtures

Christians are learning how to distinguish between members of a church and disciples of Christ. Discipleship involves developing virtues in those who come to our churches seeking life, salvation, grace, mercy. If we want to have something to offer a world in desperate need, then we must return to virtues like discernment, justice, courage, and moderation. We must return to the hard and glorious work of making disciples.

Godly Leadership

Nehemiah was called to return to Jerusalem to lead in the sacred task of rebuilding the city's walls. Displaying characteristics often lacking in secular leadership—prayerful humility, a willingness to work with diverse teams, wisdom in confronting conflict, and a passion to stand with the powerless—Nehemiah offered his people a portrait of godly leadership that can still shape our own calls to lead nearly 2,500 years later.

Galatians
Freedom in Christ

Paul wrote with fiery passion, as you will notice from the opening paragraphs of this letter to the Galatians. But his language reveals that he was writing about a crucially important issue—the very nature of salvation in Christ.

A Holy and Surprising Birth

Christmas begins here—discover these five love stories from the book of Luke and renew your appreciation of God's laborious effort to birth our salvation.

How Does the Church Decide?

An array of decisions draw energy and time from church members. These decisions may be theological, such as mode of baptism, aesthetic, such as the color of the sanctuary carpet, or functional, such as the selection of a new minister. This study will consider how the church has made its decisions in the past to help guide our decisions today.

Is God Calling?

Witness the varying forms of God's call, the variety of people called, and the variety of responses. Perhaps God's call to you will become clearer.

James
Gaining True Wisdom
If we'll be honest with God and ourselves as we study what James says, we can make great strides toward wisdom and a living faith.

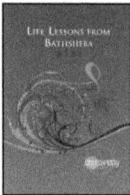

Life Lessons from Bathsheba
Who was Bathsheba? She was a complex figure who developed from the silent object of David's lust into a powerful, vocal, and influential queen mother.

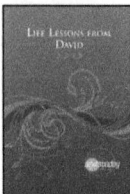

Life Lessons from David
In the Bible, we catch David in the various stages of the human journey: childhood, adolescence, adulthood, and senior adulthood. From the biblical treatment of the stages of David's life, we can land some insights to assist us in better understanding the human journey.

The Matriarchs
The matriarchs of Genesis offer their lives as a testimony of faith, perseverance, and audacity. We learn from their mistakes and suffering. We will gain the hope of Hagar, the joy of Sarah, and the audacity of Rebekah as we are challenged to examine our prejudices and our insecurities while studying Esau and Jacob's wives.

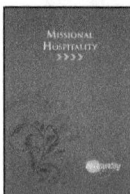

Missional Hospitality
If we are serious about following Jesus, we will be people of open hearts, open hands, and open homes. In other words, as followers of Jesus we will practice the fine art of hospitality. In lesson one, we reflect on hospitality to strangers. In lesson two, we address hospitality to the poor. In lesson three, we focus on hospitality to sinners. In lesson four, we learn about hospitality to newcomers. Lesson five reminds us about our hospitality to Christ.

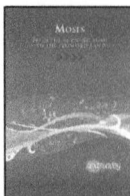

Moses
From the Burning Bush to the Promised Land
We would do well to trace the life of Moses so we might discover how his life changed, both personally and as Israel's leader, as he learned what it meant to love God with all his heart, soul, and strength.

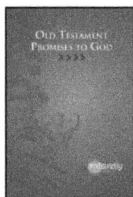

Old Testament Promises to God

Some individuals may feel that our promises couldn't possibly mean anything to God. Perhaps the real question is this: under what circumstances should or do we make such promises? The Old Testament contains several examples of people making promises to God, using the unique form of a biblical "vow."

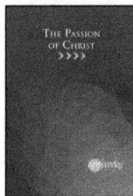

The Passion of Christ

The four lessons in this unit highlight the faith struggles of the early disciples. In lesson one, Jesus addresses the issues of faith and practice. In lesson two, we meet Judas who, like us, struggled with God's Kingdom and human kingdoms. In lesson three, the issue of temptation reminds us that our faith journey is a constant challenge. Lesson Four invites us to remember Peter's experience of "faith failure." Peter's failure, however, is not the final word. There is forgiveness.

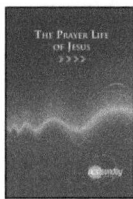

The Prayer Life of Jesus

The study of Jesus' prayer life can deepen our own prayer practices. These five sessions examine the importance of prayer at various stages of Jesus' life and ministry. He made no important decisions without consulting God.

Prepare the Way

In these sessions, we will seek to prepare the way toward and into the Christmas season. We begin with the theme of hopeful watchfulness in light of the coming of Christ. Next, we will spend two sessions considering the ministry of John the Baptist, the forerunner of Christ. Then, we will consider Matthew's account of the birth of Jesus and join in wonder at the miracle of "God with us." Finally, we will remember the story of the "holy innocents" killed by Herod in his attempt to eliminate the Christ child's threat to his power.

Proverbs for Living

Long ago, a collection of wise teachers committed themselves to the ways of God and collected this wisdom into what we know as the book of Proverbs. These four lessons explore the simple truth of Proverbs: there is a good life to be had—a life lived in faithfulness to God.

Qualities of Our Missional God

Too often we are tempted to let "numbers" drive missions. The book of Numbers reminds us that missions is motivated by something deeper. Missions reflects the heart and nature of God. If we can just get past the math, we can see God's nature clearly in the book of Numbers. . . in the wilderness.

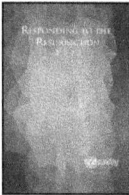

Responding to the Resurrection

All major events of human history elicit responses as varied as the personalities and situations represented by those affected. No one witnesses a world-changing event without being affected in some way. Studying the response of early followers helps us to shape our own response to the resurrection of Jesus. Each of us must consider our response to Jesus' life, teachings, death, resurrection, and call on our lives.

The Seven Deadly Sins

What exactly is sin? Just as we organize our cupboards and our schedules to make sense of our lives, Christian thinkers have organized sin into a number of categories in order to understand and surrender these patterns to God. The notion of "seven deadly sins" emerged as a way to recognize specific dangers to our spiritual lives. The purpose of the book is to guide people away from sin and into a wise and godly life.

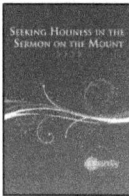

Seeking Holiness in the Sermon on the Mount

The Sermon on the Mount has long been recognized as the pinnacle of Jesus' teaching. But with this importance in mind, it's easy to think of Jesus' teachings as lofty and idealistic, offering little guidance for everyday life. Perhaps Jesus' sermon allows us to see beyond ourselves, beyond our own failures and shortcomings— revealing God's intention for our lives.

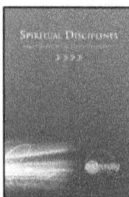

Spiritual Disciplines
Obligation or Opportunity?

The spiritual disciplines help deepen a believer's faith and increases his or her intimacy with Christ. In this study, we take a deeper look at some of the disciplines and consider their practice as a response to God's love.

Sing We Now of Christmas

In this study, we will explore some familiar prophecies, as well as the Gospel birth narratives, through the lens of five traditional Christmas carols. As carols have grown to be a fuller and more meaningful part of our worship and celebration, so too can the stories of Jesus' birth continue to grow within us and enrich our faith experience.

Stewardship
A Way of Living

Great News! Stewardship is not about money! At least not *just* about money. Certainly, stewardship relates to money, and, yes, we need to tithe. However, stewardship branches out into multiple areas of life. Properly practiced, this act of service can lead to peace and purpose in living.

The Ten Commandments

When the Ten Commandments are in the news, it is usually because a judge or teacher has hung them up on the walls. The Ten Commandments do not need to be posted or even preached nearly so much as they need to be practiced and viewed as life-giving, joyful affirmations of a better way of life.

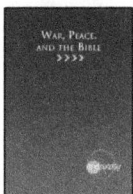

War, Peace, and the Bible

As people of faith, we are faced daily with an expectation that we participate in violent actions, our willingness to allow violence in the world to continue, and our response to violence in our lives. Is there a place for war and violence in our faith?

What Would Jesus Say?
A Lenten Study

To address what Jesus would say, we need to discover what Jesus did say. These lessons will attempt to help us understand Jesus' teachings and apply them today.

The Wonder of Easter

In 1 Corinthians 15, Paul asserts that the message that Jesus died for our sins, was buried, and rose on the third day is "of first importance" (v. 3). It is the core of the gospel story and of the Christian faith. But as much as Easter is a mystery to contemplate, it is also a hope to embrace and good news to proclaim.

**NextSunday Studies
are available from**

NextSunday
Resources

www.ingramcontent.com/pod-product-compliance
Lightning Source LLC
Chambersburg PA
CBHW070549030426
42337CB00016B/2424

Introduction II

If the Devil is reading this

I hope he enjoys

Introduction III

If you are reading this
I hope you enjoy

Jump

Unique

She had five eyes

Four noses

Three chins

And everybody laughed at her

So she gave up an eye

A nose

A chin

But everybody still laughed at her

So she gave up everything that made her her

Until she looked like everybody else

And nobody cared to notice her

Unique II

"Normalcy is a disease"
My Grandpa used to teach me
But when I tried to fake sick
With a case of being normal
My teacher simply laughed
I guess I should have learned a lesson

Lucky

I tripped on a crack

Fell onto your lap

Now I don't believe in superstitions

Impressions

"You certainly know how to make a first impression"
I didn't know what I was doing at all
But it was the best thing I've ever done

Maternal Instincts

She shivers, wrinkling her nose up at the stars
Wondering aloud if they're cold
Above the stars, the sun peers down
Hoping we're not too cold

Those Who Wait

They say good things come to

I never knew

Because I could never wait to find out who

Blue Eyes

You said I have the bluest eyes

As I swam a lap in yours

Drowned myself in yours

Lost myself in yours

Forgetting how to see

Anything but yours

Mona Lisa

Please stay still

For just this moment

So I can paint myself a memory

That can live forever

Wanderlust

My Grandma used to say "happiness is a pebbled path"
I never knew what that meant
Until I met you

When You Meet Her

When you meet her you will feel a wave of calm crash over you like a tsunami, tearing down the hopelessness inside and replacing it with splashes of sunlight and reminders of loveliness. You will not reach for your life vest to pull you above the surface, you will submerge deeper into the flooding, finding comfort.

You will realize butterflies can breathe underwater too, circling the whirlpool she has created in your gut with an excitement matching your own as a child on the first day of summer.

When you meet her you will understand why stars elect to remain above. The sun returns home nightly and whispers about the beauty she has seen, convincing the sprinkles in the sky not to fall out of fear of turning a dull shade of envy.

You will realize clouds are couches for souls that wish to live vicariously through you, having floated along, never meeting their mates. You will catch snowflakes on your fingers and watch daydreams of former loves play out until they melt away with a silent direction to follow.

When you meet her you will finally understand why the girl you insisted was the girl of your dreams in High School dumped you before college. She was not the girl of your dreams, she was one too many drinks on a Saturday night, thinking that love is found in the bottom of a bottle of Bud Light.

You will realize the girl of your dreams is in front of you, but it is a different kind of drunk. If a cop asked, you could not recite the alphabet backwards, forwards, sideways, upside down. You could not even name a letter. Asked to walk in a straight line, you would walk like a child playing don't step on the lava, dancing around to meet her eyes. If the cop asked your address, you would say cloud and he would shake his head and let you off the hook with a warning; cupid is on the loose.

When you meet her you will remember your Grandpa telling you that love feels like home. She will tear down the walls of uncertainty inside, painting murals of hands merging in bags of popcorn at the movies, drunken lips colliding on repeat, a quartet of words you wrote in the sand that leaves her lips paralyzed, but her head nodding in delight. Her eyes will be the only TV channel you wish to tune into, the sound of her car door closing and the click-clack of her heels inching towards the "welcome home" mat will sound like Beethoven's symphony. You will regret laughing as a child when your Grandpa advised you to remember the ancient proverb, "Home is where the heart lives." You will understand he was wise, as you look upon your castle of cherish.

There are 615,000 results for "I feel like my heart skipped a beat" on Google. When you meet her, you will realize why.

Cliches

It's the day dreams, the songs she sings, the wave of calm her aura brings, keeping my mind from floating to the trouble things. A blanket ever-lasting on my shoulders keeping me warm, butterflies in my stomach in a constant swarm, the last drop of rain in a thunderstorm. Cliches lining the page, all about you, rhymes that can't capture all that you do. But I will always try.

Thesaurus

I wanted to describe how beautiful you are
But couldn't find the words
So I bought a thesaurus
And you are so alluring, appealing, charming, cute,
dazzling, delicate, delightful, elegant, exquisite,
fascinating, fine, gorgeous, graceful, grand, lovely,
magnificent, marvelous, pleasing, pretty, splendid,
stunning, superb, wonderful.

I Wish To Be

I wish to be so many things. I wish to be the sunlight that awakens you in the morning. I wish to be a blanket on a snowy evening covering you from the cold. I wish to be a melody that plays over the dark thoughts that fill your brain. I wish to be a walking reminder that loneliness is no more than a persuasive stranger, and love is all around you. I wish to be a dictionary of self-help definitions. Remember, you exist. I'm so happy you exist. I wish to be the joke that makes you laugh so hard that milk shoots out of your nose. I wish to be the butterflies in your stomach when someone compliments you the right way. The way you deserve. I wish to be the crunching of the autumn leaves, the foliage that fills your eyes with magnificent colors. I wish to be the smell of a new book, the excitement to turn the page and get to the next chapter. To keep going. I wish to be the way you feel on Christmas, presents scattered underneath the tree. Knowing that people know you. Knowing that people care. I wish to be your flashlight in the darkest of places. I wish to be less cliche for you. I wish to be a safe haven from the storms that come and go. I wish to be the sun, the sky, the stars, and the moon. I wish to be everything for you.

Jump

They asked if I would jump off a bridge if you did first
Truth is I would jump first
To test the water, to make sure it isn't too cold
To ensure you land safely
To serve as a trampoline, lifting you back up
To fall for you one last time
Even if you change your mind

Slip Into The Void With Me

You loathe the summer sun
She burns your sensitive skin
I complain about the winter winds
As they mock the mess we're in

Your daddy issues go on display
Every time you date
So when I drunk call about my Mother
You believe in fate

Despite shaky hands and blackened minds
We can always see the light
So I guess we're teaching one another
Two wrongs must make a right

They say misery loves company
So let's take a table for two
We can laugh away our demons
Until they're laughing too

Rainbow

Roses are red

Violets are blue

I could not find a more cliche way

To say how I appreciate you

Roses are red

Violets are blue

I saw in black and white

Until I met you

Roses are red

Violets are blue

Now I embrace my colors

And hope to shine like you

Grey Skies

We huddled beneath the awning
As the rain cried down
The sky was airing its grievances
Yet I couldn't hide my smile
Winds roared at my trembling legs
But it was you who blew me away

Maps

I used to fear losing my way
I forged the same path every day
Until one time I saw a face
Made me change my entire pace
Now no clue where to go
Only fear, but this I know
There is so much beauty in your blues
I'd learn the way just for you

The Church of You

I spent 18 years attending church

Listening to Gospels

But the smile you slip between our lips greeting

Is what leads me to believe

Blonde

Fall on my shoulders

In a warm embrace

Find comfort on my pillow

On my jacket

Anywhere and everywhere

Until I brisk you away

Always hoping for more

If I Leave You On Read

Odds are I've been swallowed by the moon

Swept up by the stars

Stunned by the sights and sounds

Or by the warmth of her lips

The glow of her eyes

The soothing hum of her voice

I will not be asleep

I will be the next day's sunrise

Skeleton

My hands tremble

My bones are brittle

My skin is thin

But when you embrace me

There is no body I would rather call home

Safety Net

Though I am slender and shaky

You must understand

I can be your steady hands

Chorus

My heart sings the loveliest song when I see you

I hope you can hear it too

Home

It was a quarter past far too late
And I asked you to take me home
So we didn't move an inch

To Be Continued I

Appreciate the good times

The next wave won't wait

I hope you've found a poem you like

Before it gets too late

If you wish to venture ahead, go forth

But I must tell you this

The poems ahead speak of broken hearts

Not a lover's kiss

Burn

Stung

I stopped to smell the roses

And got stung by a bee

Chicago

How strange it was to learn
That you could be in my arms
Fitting together so perfectly
Yet even in that moment
You felt miles away

Disenchanting

After our first date I wrote you a poem

And you said you loved it

And you showed it to all of your friends

After our third date I wrote you a poem

And you said you loved it

And you shared it online

After I asked you to be mine I wrote you a poem

And you said you loved it

And you showed it to your Mom and Dad

After our first fight I wrote you a poem

And you said you appreciated it

And you kept it to yourself

After I didn't see you for the holidays I wrote you a
poem

And you said it was nice of me to do that

And you never told me what you did with it

Last week I wrote you a poem

And you said you would get around to it

And you never read it at all

Thesaurus II

I threw away my thesaurus
I don't want to describe you anymore

The Sun

The sun is no different than you or I

She wishes to embrace

But if she gets too close

Everyone burns

Rotten

Often it feels

I am pulling your weeds

From my skin

So I can be my own garden

And finally grow

Suffocation

I love you

Do you love me?

I love that you love me

Do you still love me?

I love that

Is everything okay?

Okay

I wish you still loved me

Summer

Blooming flowers wilt beneath your feet

Your boots crushed the last of them

I picked you a dandelion to make you smile

And the wind blew it away

Unspoken Farewell

You sneak softly into the night
Footsteps failing to make a sound
I awake to find you gone
Beginning diverging paths

Yet as you forge your own way
I do not seek re-connection
I do not wonder
I remain

A Storm Brews

I bottle my anger and send it to Sea

Only to see it hurled back

"I am not a home for untold rage,"

She cries

"Don't you ever wonder how storms begin?"

Accident

You are the mud stuck to the sole of my shoe

I am a U-turn into heavy traffic

You are dragging me through uneven sidewalks

I am spinning out of control

Tick Tock

Tick tock

The clock is running laps and I cannot keep up

Tick tock

My throat is on fire with words unspoken

Tick tock

I'm sorry it took me two drinks

Tick tock

To spill two years

Tick tock

But when we were golden

Tick tock

I swear time stood still

Tick tock

And I long to linger on your lips once more

Tick tock

But our time has passed

Wicker

One day under neon lights
Drunk on wine and in a haze
We will find each other smoking cigarettes
Neither of us smoke but it will feel like fate
With warning signs fixed across our foreheads
But maybe your lips will smell like strawberry
And mine bubblegum
Almost enough

Perhaps the past will sit as a shadow
Holding a boombox above its head
Incredibly cliche
Incredibly us
But slowly
Like a candle gasping for one last breath
Together
We will melt

Whisper

Whisper my name
In between smoky breaths
Your lips emit
It's winter

Whisper my name
Into my ear
Like it's gospel
Like it's spring

Whisper my name
A firefly's song
That lost its tempo
At the end of summer

Whisper my name
So I can remember
What once lingered
Before the fall

Parasite

I offered you a piece of me
And you took and you took and you took
From all I was

So I re-grew as a parasite
And I took and I took and I took
From everyone else

So I crawled through seeping skin
And I bit and I ticked and I stole
Until there was no one left

So I saw only the creature in the mirror
And I stopped and I shifted and I reanimated
Until I was a butterfly

And now harmless I roam free

Who Am I?

I am
Detaching from my skin
Hollowed out like a shell
on sand

I am
Accepting apologies
That never escaped your
lips

I am
Stars
Seeing stardust in self-
inflicted wounds

I am
A flower
On the tombstone of who
you made me be

I am
Questions
Can I do it? Can I make it
through?

I am
Answers
I can do it. I am enough.

I am
The tattoo on the lower
lip of your back
Belonging to you

I am
Begging you to stay
While showing you the
door

I am

More myself than I will

ever be you

My own flesh and blood

I am

Leaving you behind

For the flowered road

ahead

Hearing Things

Tonight I swear I heard your voice
A faint whisper between gusts of wind
"Are you okay?"
I felt tireless

Tonight I saw the sun rattling her cage
But the dull, grey gate budged not
Drops of snowflaked tears fell from the sky
I felt cold

Tonight I heard winter roaring in laughter
Reminiscing tales of nights spent alone
Tales of nights inside my head
I felt weak

Tonight I learned to sleep without song
Tonight I shined, myself a light
Tonight I am existing everywhere
Tonight I am strong

A Suicide Note

His lips where mine belong

Inferno

What do I think of?
Burning buildings
I saw

In your eyes
Looking down
When I made you blush

Does he notice?
You laugh like a child
When you're high

Atop burning building
Looking down
On me

Trying to sleep
With vacancy
Wondering

If you are a ghost

And I am a ghost

Can we see each other?

Fragments

There is nothing left

                                    You stole

Every piece of me

                                    I loved

The way you peeled from my lips to sneak a smile
Thinking I wouldn't notice

                                    I noticed

There is nothing left

                                    You stole

Every memory of you

                                    I dreaded

The way you peeled them from my skin
Until into torn up polaroids

                                    I fell apart

Momentos

How strange it is

To sit in a shoebox beneath your bed

As you lie stoic in a picture frame

Beneath old poems I never got to read to you

Not Us, Not Us, Not Us

Not us, not us, not us. How could we fall apart?. We were invincible. We were a tidal wave crashing over anyone that dared to doubt us. We were weeknights spent lying under the covers, ignoring the thunderbolts being thrown between my mother and father beneath us. I didn't realize love could be sunlight until I met you. We were Friday nights in the fall spent jumping in leaves, laughing as if we were kids again. Saturday nights spent floating around parties, mixing love and liquor into a perfect haze. Sunday nights spent with my Grandpa, listening to his tales of past love and how forever could be real, trust him, he knows from experience. Forever could be us. I never felt warmer than when he would speak and you would listen.

Listen, you said. You never started sentences like that, you were always bubbling with concepts and smiles, so when your voice dropped an octave and your eyes looked dull, I knew something was off. You told me things had changed, you were seeing things differently and I wasn't in your field of view.

Through all the streetlights and star-brights, the neon signs on stores we used to hold hands in, I saw memories, you could only see a dead end now.

Now the memories slip through the cracks in my head like sand through an hourglass, I can no longer remember whether you were drinking milk or water when i made you laugh so hard your nose flooded I can no longer remember your brother's favorite movie that I watched with him only to get closer to you.

Your aunt, the one with the purple hair, Alice, right? No maybe Annette. Right, Annette. That has to be it. When she met me, she told me to enjoy it while it lasted. I never understood why she would say something like that at a dinner party. I wanted to know what happened to her to make her that cold to a stranger filled with nothing but love and maybe a little bit of wine.

Now I understand she was a highway sign, flashing "DANGER AHEAD" but I was too busy looking at the passenger seat to listen.

Now we drive under the sky, our souls vacant beneath the black and blue.

Black and blue, the colors discovered when your Father's fist met my eye. I expected a handshake, but when he saw my clothes on your floor and my lips on your neck he wanted to unglue me the only way he knew how. He never gave me a second chance, but please tell him I'm sorry for the mess I left behind for him. I wish I could have been around longer to help. I remember the battle that waged between you two when he found out you were still dating me a few months later. World War 3 has already happened, and it sounds like your Father's bombastic instruction telling you not me, mixed with your cries, "you can't do this to us! Not us. Not us. Not us." Not us. You were right, he couldn't do it to us. We were invincible, remember? I wrote a story the other night out of the blue. The words arrived in my head like they had been sitting in a queue, waiting to flow onto the pages. The story is about a girl who thought she was unlovable, she was more familiar with teardrops and shot glasses than arms around her or expressions of admiration. The story is about a boy who used to be able to speak novels to that girl, the same one that looked at him like he was the answer to a question that was always lingering in her mind. Now he speaks in short stories, always getting cut off before the good part of the story.

The story starts with a beginning, he's drawn in by her vibrant eyes at a party, and rushes over with a line to win her affection. He trips over his words and trips over a crack in the sidewalk, spilling them all over her until her dress is soaked and he's told her everything he's seen. She gives him a kiss on the cheek and he has to look down at his shoes because he feels he must be melting. They spend the night laying on a field underneath the stars, as cliche as can be, but they don't care. On her lips he can taste stardust. In her eyes he can see the moonlight. They entangle on top of the world.

The climax is my favorite part, the boy and the girl are a modern day Romeo and Juliet. In her ears, he whispers "I look for you in everyone," In his ears, she whispers "I'm always thinking about you." In her dreams she sees him as a cowboy, lassoing away her demons with a smile, "not today boys." Together, they like to skip rocks and say they're only a stone's throw away, knowing they will never feel alone.

Together they must be invincible.

The end is where I struggle. No one ever told me that Romeo and Juliet die in the end. No one ever told me that forever for one is not forever for another, or that looking to the passenger seat and seeing an imprint leftover from the night she said goodbye would finally cause him to melt. She says she doesn't really think about him anymore. Her demons are on the loose, She says she's been having night terrors, she's seeing someone new now, Insomnia. Insomnia knows the boy only as a great threat, so Insomnia sneakily slips stones into the pockets of the relationship. then sends it to the lake.

I wrote this story the other night and my editor returned it with a picture of us splashed across the cover. "The story of us" he wants me to call it.

Please tell me it's not an autobiography. We were invincible, remember? We were invincible. Come back to me, I know you're there. Come back to me, these bones are too fragile to carry the weight of missing you.

Come back to me, I want to tear the pages of this story out and set them on fire, but my lighter is still in your bedroom drawer. Come back to me, we can make a bonfire out of it together and laugh until enough tears come out to extinguish the flame. Remember, like we used to? Come back to me, please don't let this story be about us. Not us, not us, not us.

To Be Continued II....

Before it gets worse

There is a calming wave

I hope this makes you smile

Radiate

This Little Light of Mine

We are not our mothers, we are not our fathers

We are not mistakes, their mistakes

They made decisions, selfish decisions

A house is not always a home

A parent is not inherently golden

I will radiate despite her

Millennials

The future is a tattoo parents never approved

The future is a protest sign peeking out of the
huddled masses

The future skipped class to attend a lecture on
feminism

The future bought earplugs for Thanksgiving dinner

The future hears your statement, but raises you a
question

It's what you taught us, show your work

The future will not stop until the question has been
answered

The future will not be patronized

Your experiences are not universal

The future is terrified of what you've done

But the future is determined

The future will be okay

High

Father's screams blast louder than blaring stereos

Mother's pacing moves like the beat

Hazy eyes cannot fall in rhythm

Because a bag of Cheetos sounds like your favorite

song

Marathon

He asked me to run a mile in his shoes
So I slipped on his raggedy life
Seeing questions hale from the sky
Feeling a weight drop on my shoulders
Dragging me down
As I readied myself to run through the storm
I finally understood

Blooming

There's a garden outside my grandfather's apartment
With flowers hopelessly clinging to life
When I arrive with a can they cannot muster any
tears
Nor whisper a thank you
But I know they will be okay

The colors drain and the leaves wither as they are left
Dark like the sky when the sun leaves to sleep
Yet the sun rises again and hope holds her hand
And I know the flowers will refresh and grow again
Everything will be okay

Supernova

They told me of a star

That exploded into a light so bright

It was nearly an entire galaxy

I hope that's how I go

Begin Again

Maybe memories you once thought infinite are as fleeting as the moon at dawn, maybe nostalgia is the only lover that will stay the night, maybe your hands tremble at the thought of trying to identify yourself in this never ending maze. That's okay. The clock always strikes midnight. Every day is a new life.

Simplicity

I hope you learn the innocence of a child
The imagination of the naive
The creativity of an open book
One that needs a story

I hope you learn simplicity
No impossibilities
No impracticalities
Only poetry in motion

Mixtape

I will learn every song on every instrument

If it will get you out of bed

I will write you self help song books

If it would make a difference at all

I will embrace the calluses on my hands

If that's what it takes to kickdrum your heartbeat

I will be the mixtape you play on a rainy day

And I will never skip a beat

Decisions

Twinkle twinkle little star
Show me where the good things are
Point me in the way to go
Just this once I'd love to know

When my compass turns to dust
When I can't, but I must
Twinkle twinkle little star
Show me where the good things are

To The Girl On The Suicide Hotline

I told myself I was calling you because I had nothing
better to do.
I told myself I was calling you because the last
episode of Rocket Power was over, and a phone call
with a stranger sure as hell beat an episode of Ren &
Stimpy.
I told myself I was calling you because maybe *you*
needed someone to talk to.
I told myself a lot of things.
Maybe that's why I called you.

To the girl on the suicide hotline,
I'm sorry I never got your name.
It's just when I started to speak my mouth drooled
out waves of depression I never knew existed.
Suppressed memories cascaded into conversation like
they had been sitting in a queue.

My lungs emitted every word I locked away from my
therapist.
I'm sorry I forgot to ask how you found the key.

To the girl on the suicide hotline,
Thank you for listening to my mixtape of grievances.
I cried all the words that lingered.
"I'm tired of performing autopsies for lost
friendships."
"I'm tired of attending funerals of relationships that
died without leaving notes."
"I'm tired of mourning living people."
You asked how long I'd been tired and I couldn't
catch my breath to answer.
I expected you to disappear into thin air, a magic
trick so many performed before.

To the girl on the suicide hotline,
When you began rattling off possible solutions to me,
my hockey senses tingled.
I was a defenseman, combatting each method of self-
help you shared.

But you were a freight train of help coming and I an ant on the tracks.

You spoke of writing as a saving grace, of my brother's smile I must have slipped into the pocket of conversation when depression wasn't looking, of the way my grandfather lit up when Frank Sinatra's voice filled the airwaves. You spoke until I caught my breath.

To the girl on the suicide hotline,
I never knew that CPR could be performed through spoken words.
I never knew that empathy could stitch together open wounds.
I never knew that a stranger would introduce me to hope.
We've been steady for three years now.
I can't believe it's been three years now.

To the girl on the suicide hotline,
I'm sorry I hung up before thanking you.
I'm sorry I hung up before learning your name.

But it's just like you said,
I had a lot to get out of bed for.
I have a lot to get out of bed for.

Shrink

A Christmas Story

It's Christmas and you're celebrating
With your Father
Who left your Mother
When he found out what she did
He still sings carols all the same

It's Christmas and you're celebrating
With your friend
Who sees herself the devil
While her halo faintly flickers
Opening fits with excitement

It's Christmas and you're celebrating
With strangers
Making small talk in shallow voices
Their stories linger in the winter air
As they wear their holiday spirit disguises

It's Christmas and you're celebrating
With anyone at all

That there's 7 billion people living different plots

And everyone is alone

So no one is on their own

Father?

Answer my call
When I am desperate
Abandon me
When I am not

Write your list of demands
On the back of a funeral program
For children
Gone too soon

   forbid I slip
   forbid i sin
Or I must get on my knees
Or I must bare my soul

I wonder where hypocrisy falls
Among the devilish deeds
I wonder where I fall
For being a stranger

But the word says you love

And it's proclaimed you forgive

So tell me dear

Why must I ache so?

Truths and Lies in Troubled Times

Pour it down your throat like a bottle of bleach, swirl it around until you choke on it. It's a bitter pill you can't stand to swallow, but hey, the lump in your throat has been lonely lately. Cover your self-inflicted wounds with bandages, tell your friends what the devil on your shoulder whispered in your ear when they ask why you're bleeding. Wonder where the angel went. Make sure to check in with regret on an hourly basis, she worries you'll do something smart. Circle back with your insecurities, they know you'll do what they want. "How do you feel?" used to be such an easy question, but with your throat slammed shut all you can do is fake a smile.

Re-Done

I am no more than piled up bodies

Corpses of my former selves

Discarded attempts at existence

You held no funerals

You mourned no losses

You cried no tears

I used to be my own self

But don't you worry

You taught me better than that

Validation

You take it from a friend
Leaving them with no choice
But to medicate your self-doubt
But to blindly give

The mirror stares, frowning
At the freckle you named Judas
The one who steals
The one who makes you beg

Perhaps you're cowered in a corner
At a party
At a concert
In the bathroom of a local bar

You see swaying arms and smiling faces
Making it look so easy
It's never felt half as easy
You plead for it to be easy

One day it will be yours

Like a love that kickdrums your heart

Like a song that snugs across your eardrums

Like the feeling when you give it to someone else

Mixtape II

Take my favorite song

Forget its name

Mess up the lyrics

Sing it out of key

Like what you've done to me

Toy Story

Talk me down into your playsize toy
Dress me down in spewed criticisms
"Can't you do anything right?"
Leave me alone, naked

Make sure to place me down abruptly
With force
Rattle my bones
With disgust

You know you can
You know I'll be sitting there when you return
You promise me you'll be back soon
Just like old times

First you break the promise
Then you break me
Leaving me to piece myself back together
Until you're ready to play once more

Prayer

A child's legs knelt on a pew
Starting conversation with distant stranger
Told his response would not come through word
He waited

A boy's legs quivered under a desk
Like on a cold night, like under a weight far too heavy
Once told his response would not come through word
He waited

A man's skin smeared scarlet
As a desperate plea for attention
Once told his response would come not through word
He waited

At the bar sits a man who has not been heard
His voice shrunk into a whisper
No longer willing to wait for a response, he pleads
"When do I get to be happy?"

Labels

Your best friend's words leave you squeamish

She laughs at the weight you bear

You laugh along

Choking on your confessions

Shrinking into a shadow, black and white

Caution tape shielding your colors

Clipped Wings

I am no more than a flustered bird

Fluttering about

On my good days I fly

To the highest highs

Immersed in the bluest skies

But when skies are grey

And I have a bad day

My wings hesitate

And fault

So all I do is fall

White and Blue

He sits in a crowded basement
Sweat cascading down his neck
Hostile eyes strangling common sense
He sees a reflection of his younger self
His nose is bloody too

When he was a child he cried at needles
Until his Father stroked his hair
"It's going to be alright, son"
Now he thinks his Father a liar
And doesn't shed a tear

Vacancy

I am grasping at painted wrists
Like lotto tickets
All scratched up

You are grabbing the wheel
As I swerve around potholes
You swear do not exist

We are stuck in black and white
Colorblind
Trying to stay alive

Unwelcome

His hands find my shoulders
I shrink into a child once more

Snakes

Do not bite the hand that feeds you
It may be poisoned
Do not grasp for familiar hands
They may be calloused, they may be cold

Anxiety

SometimesIfeelliketheworldismovingtooquicklyforme
andeveryonearoundmeismovingattheirowncomfortab
lepacefloatinglikenothingcanhurtthemlikenothinghas
everhurtthembeforebutIamspeedingfrompointAtopoi
ntBtryingnottobelatetryingnottolooktoorattledtryingn
ottoletanyonedownwhenallIwanttodois B R E A T H E
butIneverlearnedhowtoslowdownIneverlearnedhowt
oletthingssimplybehowtoletmyselfbewhoIwantobeeve
nifthatmeanssomethings s l o w i n g d o w n
formyownsakeforthesakeofmysanityforthesakeofmyli
feforthesakeofmywritingandIknowIneedto r e l a x
andrememberthatIamonlyhumanIamonlyonepersonI
amdoingthebestIcanandthatiswhatcountssoasIthinka
boutthatIcanfinally learn to slow down to the right
pace and be me.

Mumble

You said you could barely hear me and that didn't surprise me at all because I lost my voice when I was a child and never found a way to get it back.

Dissociate

I am somewhere inside myself

Wandering yet again

I am searching for myself

Wondering yet again

Where I go

Bittersweet

Like a goodbye you never saw coming

Like an embrace that took you by surprise

Like your first love getting married

Like your next love meeting your eyes

Like a song you can't quite get out of your head

Like a song you never want to leave your head

A strange, familiar feeling

Bittersweet

High II

Your brain is filled with dirt

You forgot my birthday

You baked me a cake of spiders

I didn't know what to say

Your brother pulled me to the side

Said "hey dude, I like this vibe but I don't like you"

You were somewhere in the stars

I didn't know how to pull you down

Your brother was over the moon

I didn't know if I should pull him down

I never liked needles much

But I sure liked you

Atrophy

Your skin and eyes held a competition
To see which could paint themselves grayer
And they both won
So everybody lost

Ribs

They gave you your rib in a glass jar

As a token

For being broken

You kept it on your nightstand

So every time she would come over

She was reminded

She never had all of you

Your Ex-Lover Is Alive

I saw your Father sitting by an oak tree
Crouched over
Picking at dead flowers alone

I saw your Mother at the liquor store
Preparing for a party
We both know she'll drink too much at

I saw your sister at the restaurant
She was a hostess
But she still wouldn't meet my eyes

I swear I saw you in the clouds
I went to text you
And remembered I could not anymore

Let Me Tell You About My Best Friend

The first time I saw you, you were so, so stoned, sipping on a glass of whiskey, telling me how wonderful sobriety could be. You always spoke in contradictions, explaining the beauty of what you would not do for yourself. When I told you I was scared, you said you didn't know the feeling.

I remember the time you climbed down the neighbor's fence and pierced your forearm along the way. As the blood slowly swam down your wrist, you laughed about how you were as high as the stars and couldn't feel it anyway. Every time I stopped speaking, you asked me if I lost my voice. You always did the talking anyway.

I remember the time we went to the concert and you jumped right into the middle of the mosh pit. Intoxicated by the moment and several shots of your favorite beer, you blended in like you had been there for the entire night. You said the room was spinning like your favorite record and you didn't want the moment to stop.

The last time I saw you, we were quietly gazing up at the stars. You were high above the milky way, eyes redder than the blood that still sits stained on my neighbor's fence. You spoke quietly, saying you were scared. I heard the words, but I didn't understand what they meant until I couldn't tell which star was yours.

When I saw you inanimate for the first time, your Father patted me on the shoulder. He asked me how I was feeling, so I said I was scared. He told me he knew the feeling all too well.

Thank You For Reading

If you read these poems

Or even just one

I hope you are okay

If you read none at all

I hope you are okay

You are not alone

You will never be alone

Thank you for reading

About the Author

I started writing poetry when I attended Hofstra University during my sophomore year of college. I took a Creative Writing course taught by Professor Robert Plath which changed my understanding of writing and how enjoyable it could be.

In the ensuing four years I would write poems whenever they came to mind, often about what was happening in my life, but sometimes about subjects that I felt inspired to attempt to capture.

The first poem I wrote in this collection was When You Meet Her, and at no point did I write a poem for the sake of writing a poem.

I could not tell you what's coming next for me, but I'm excited to see what it is. Thank you for reading!

www.ingramcontent.com/pod-product-compliance
Lightning Source LLC
Chambersburg PA
CBHW070518030426
42337CB00016B/2012